COLORING BOOK
FOR TWEENS
FASHION GIRLS

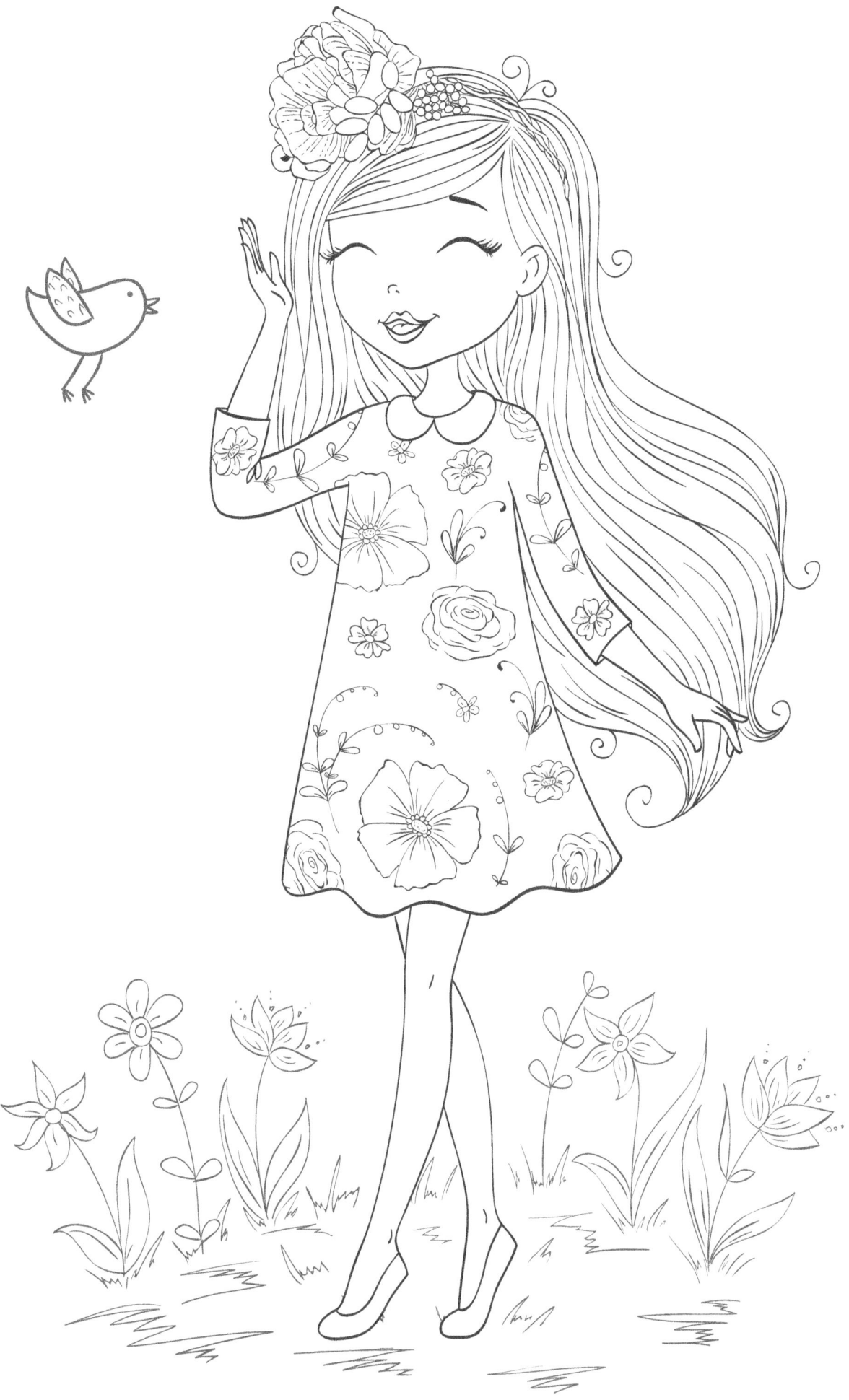

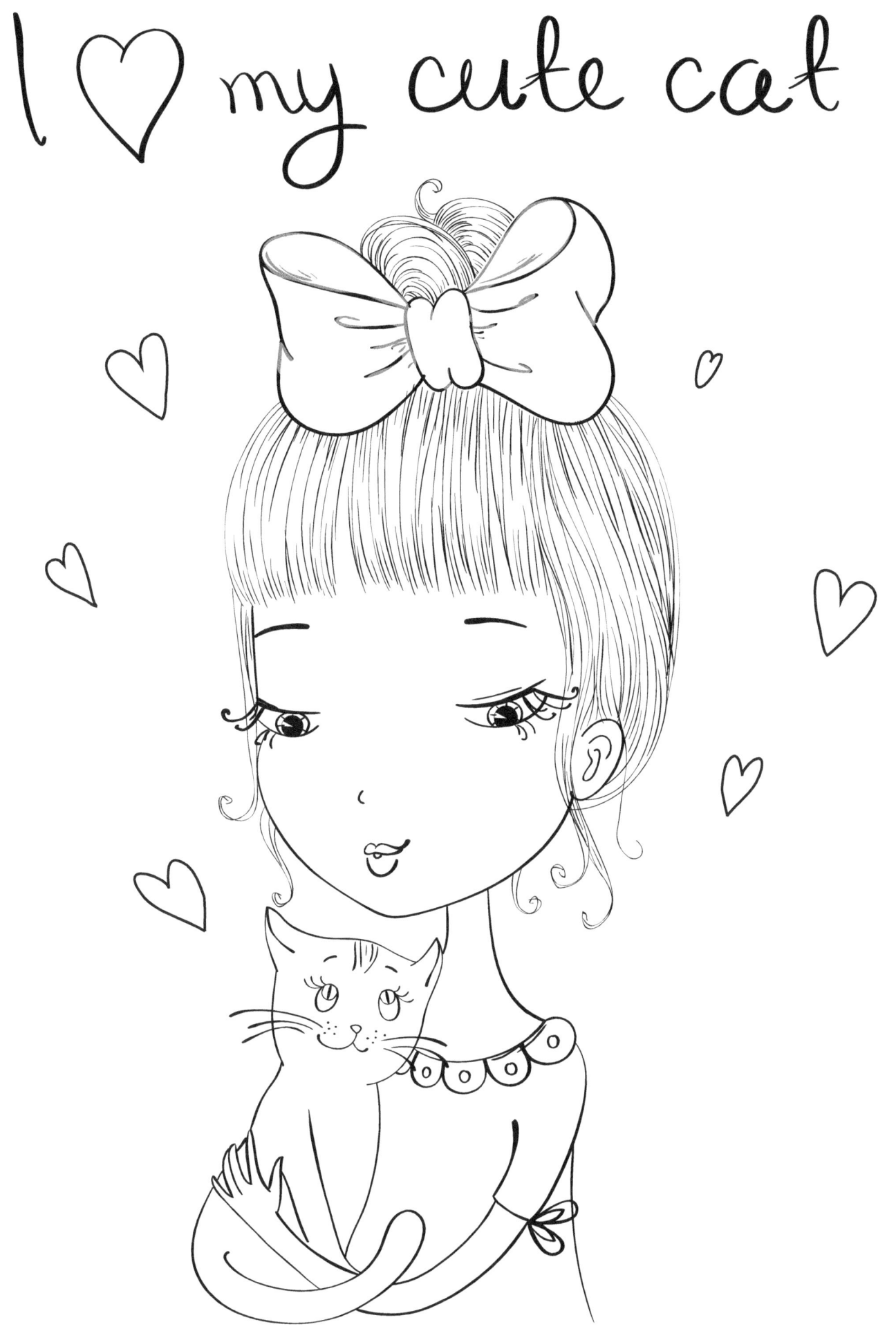

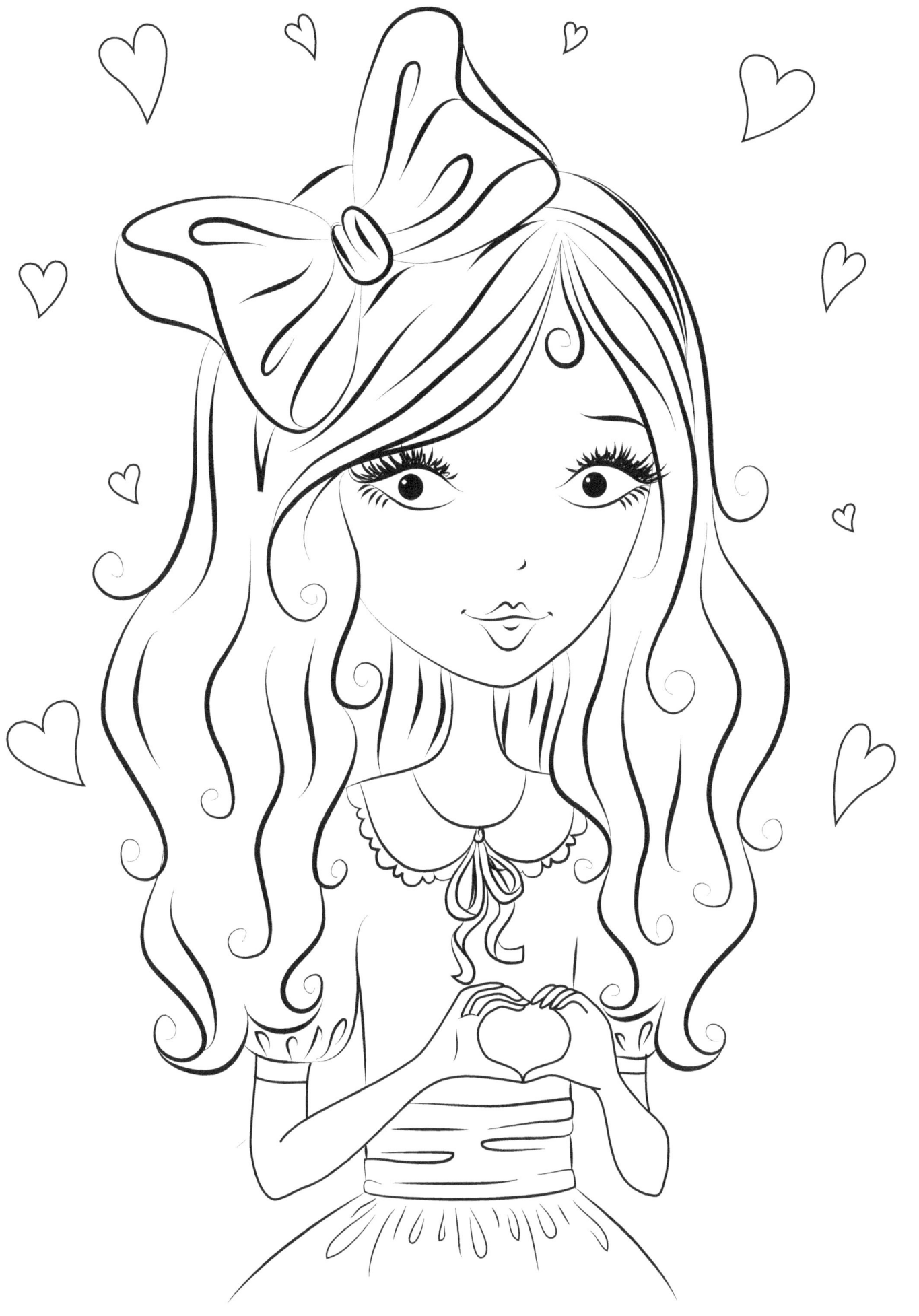

I ♥ my
Dog

best friends

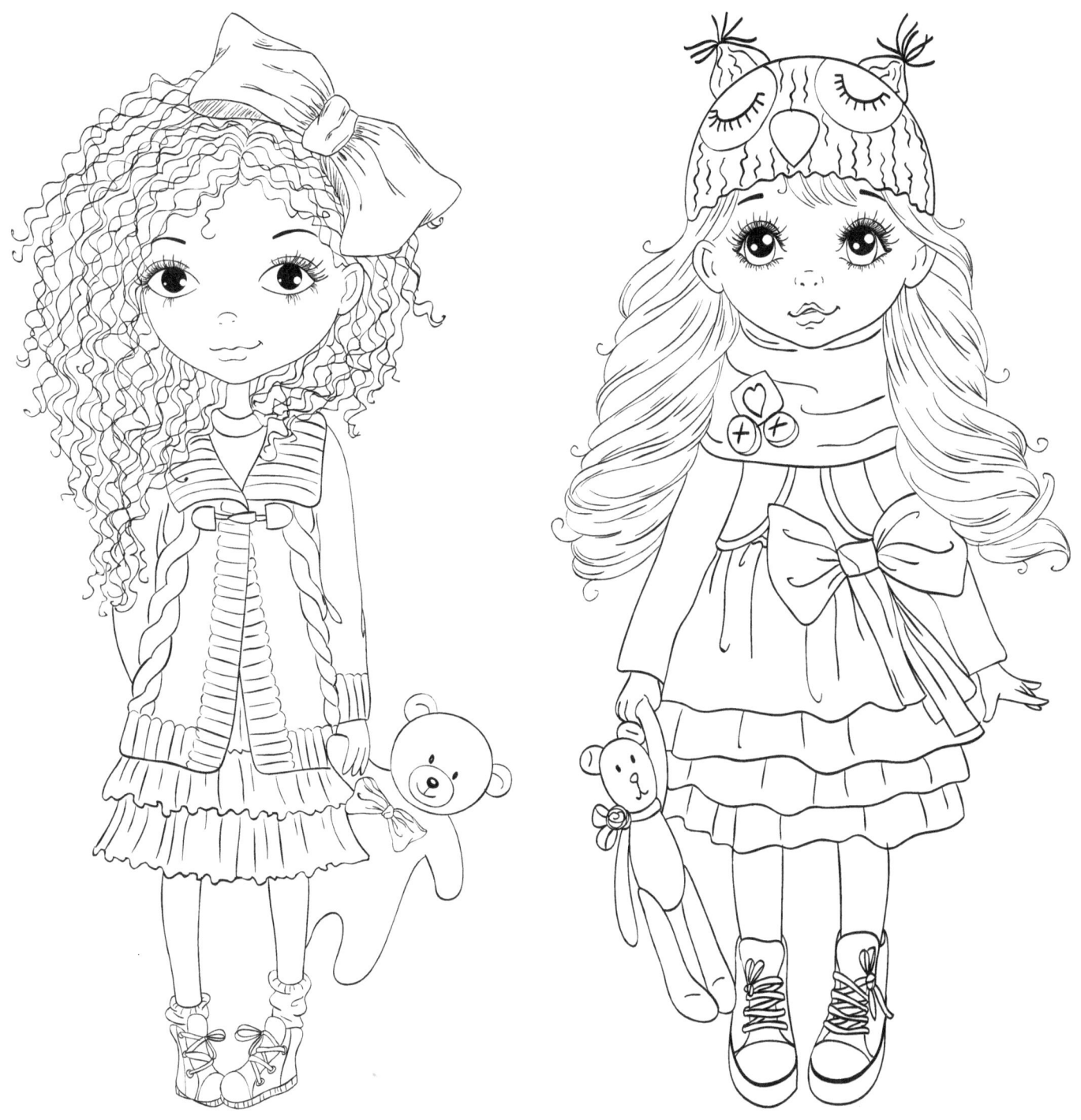

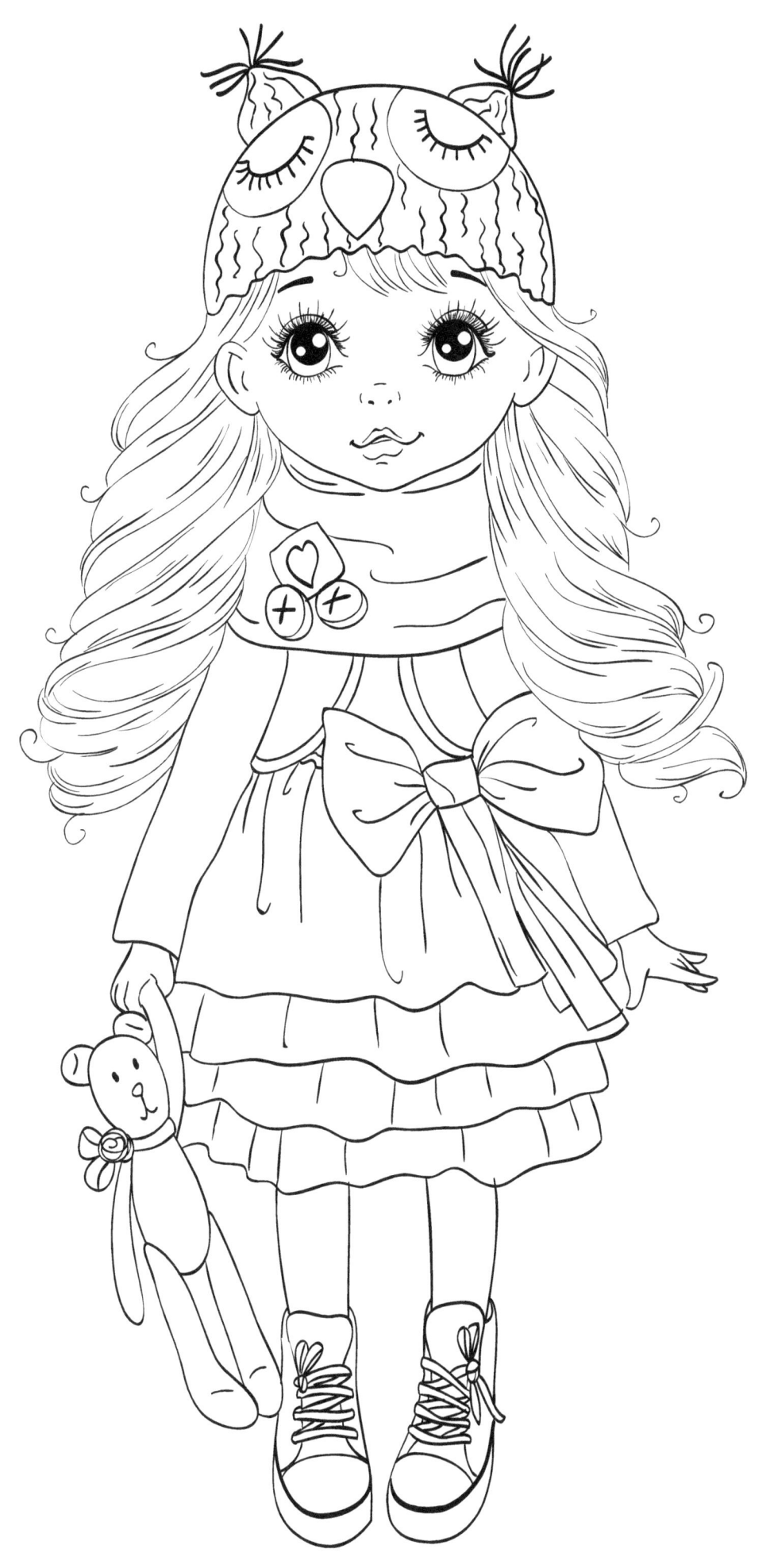

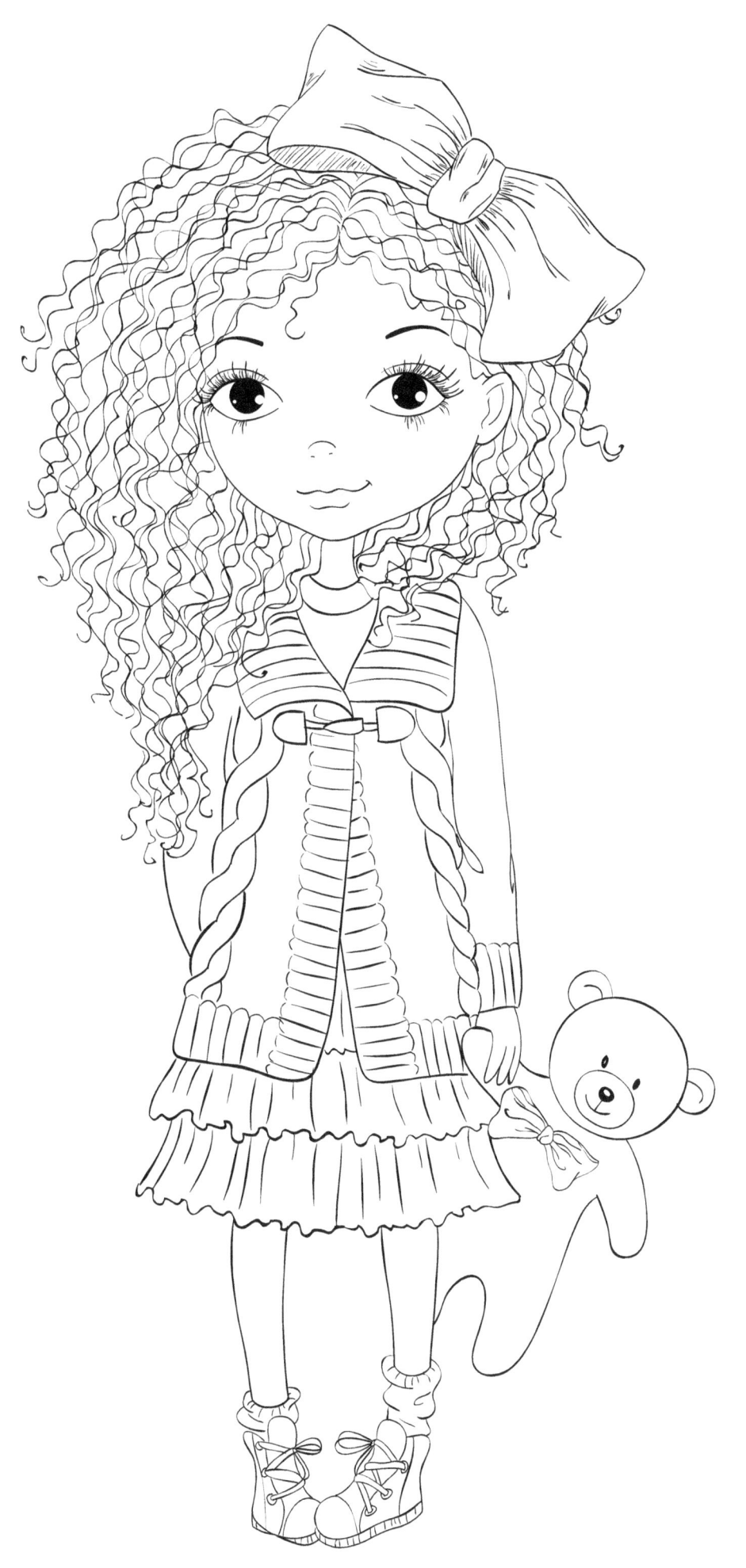

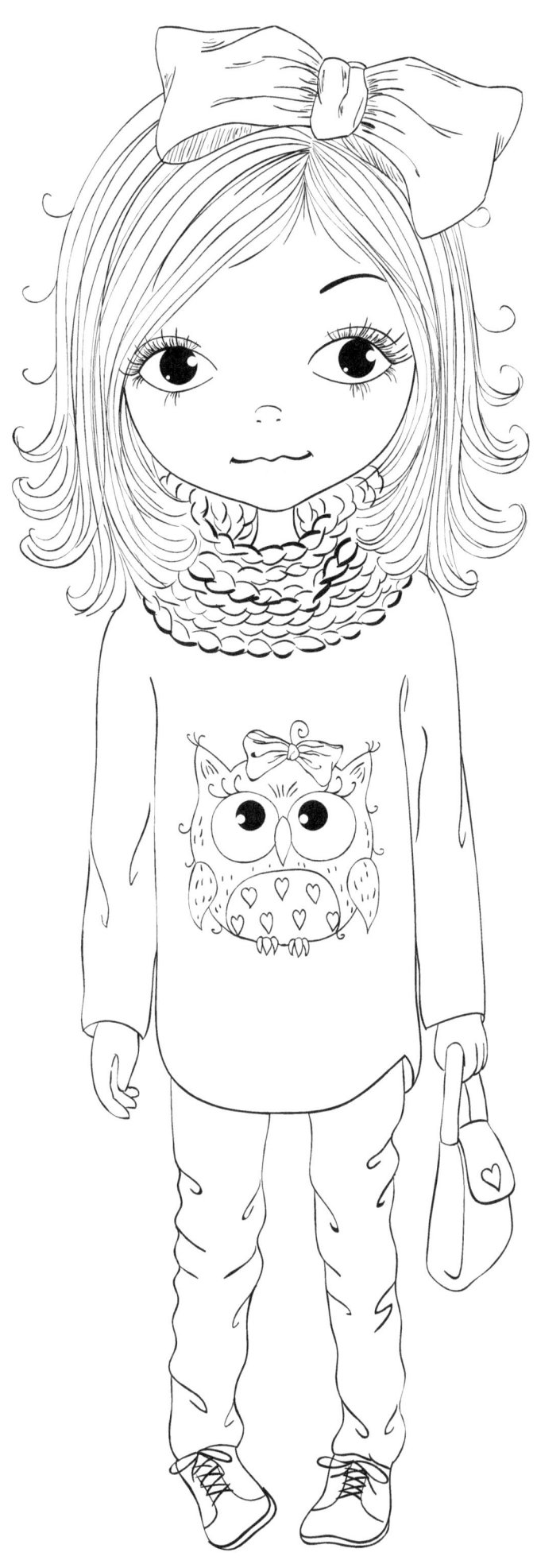

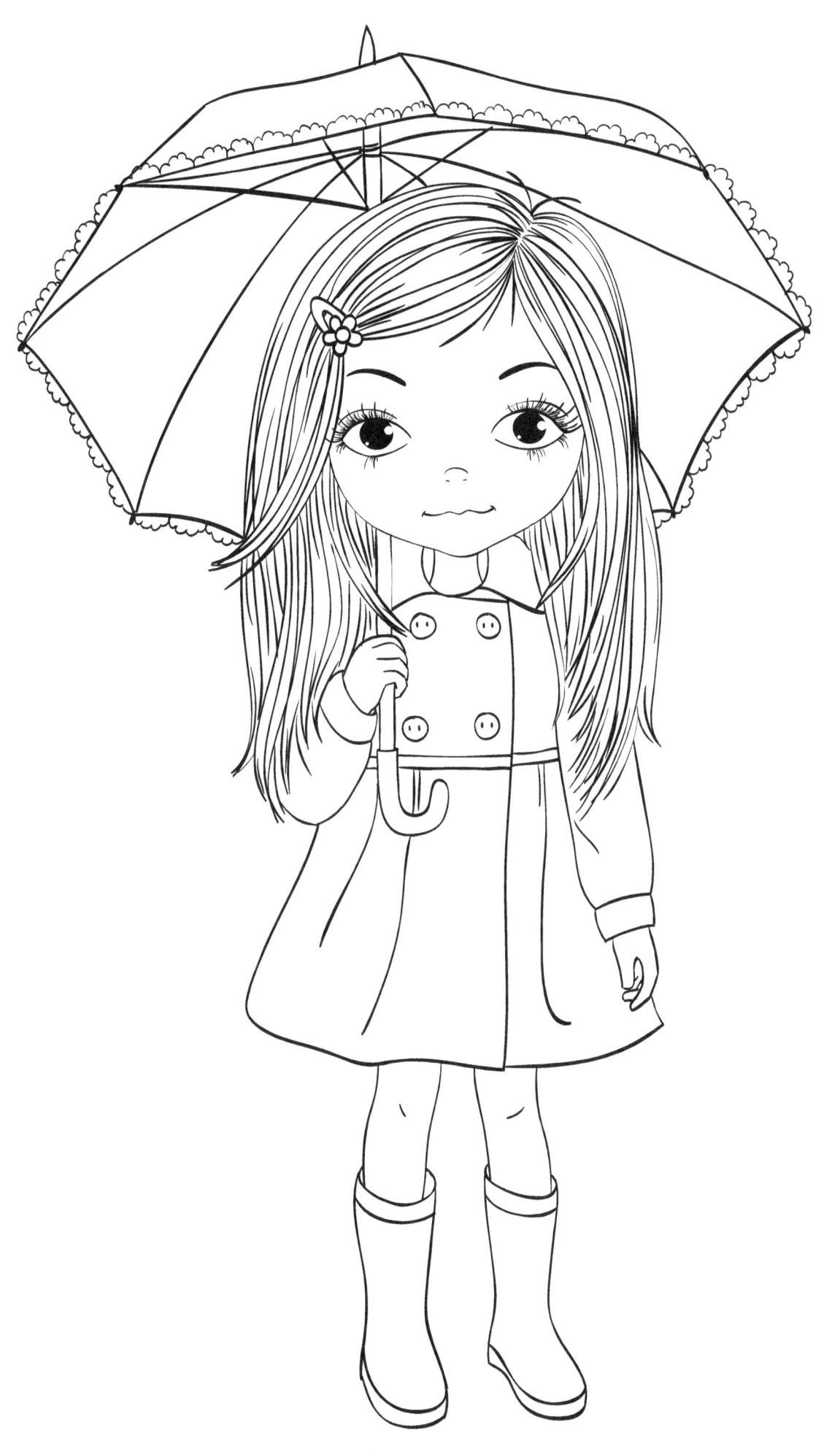

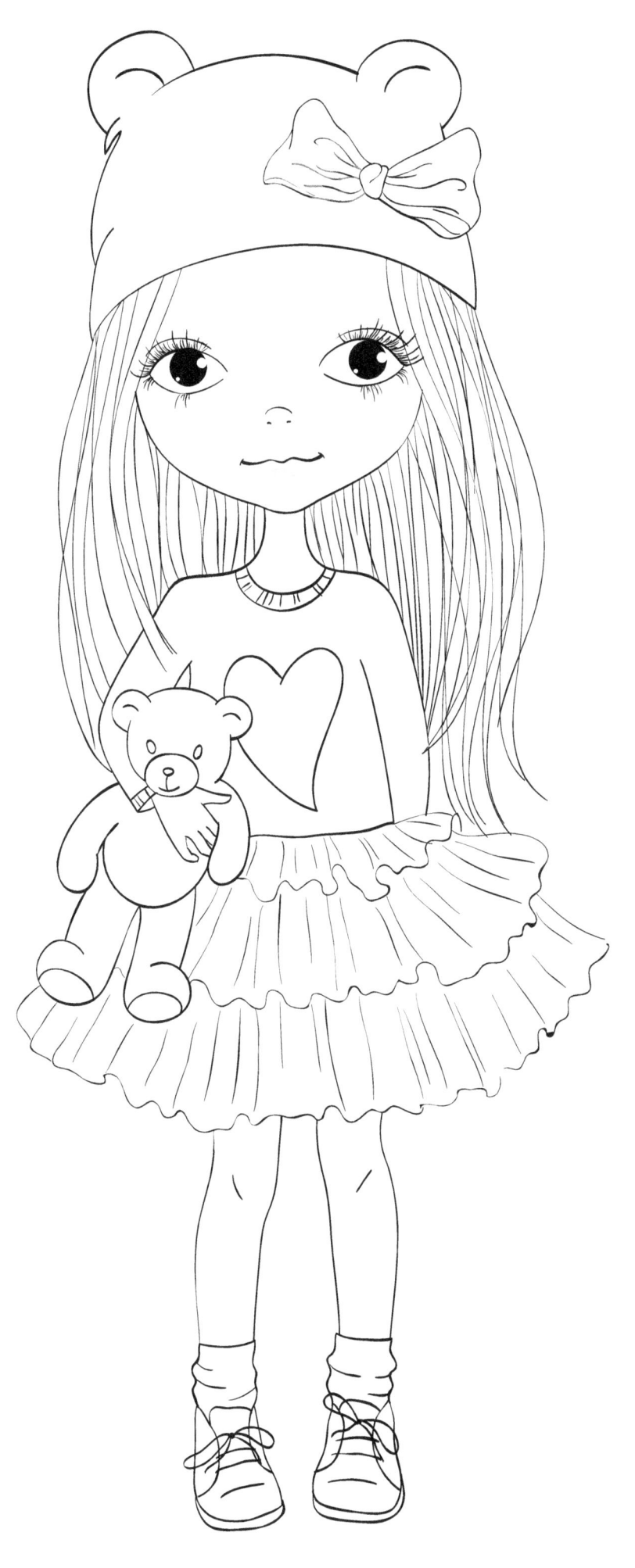

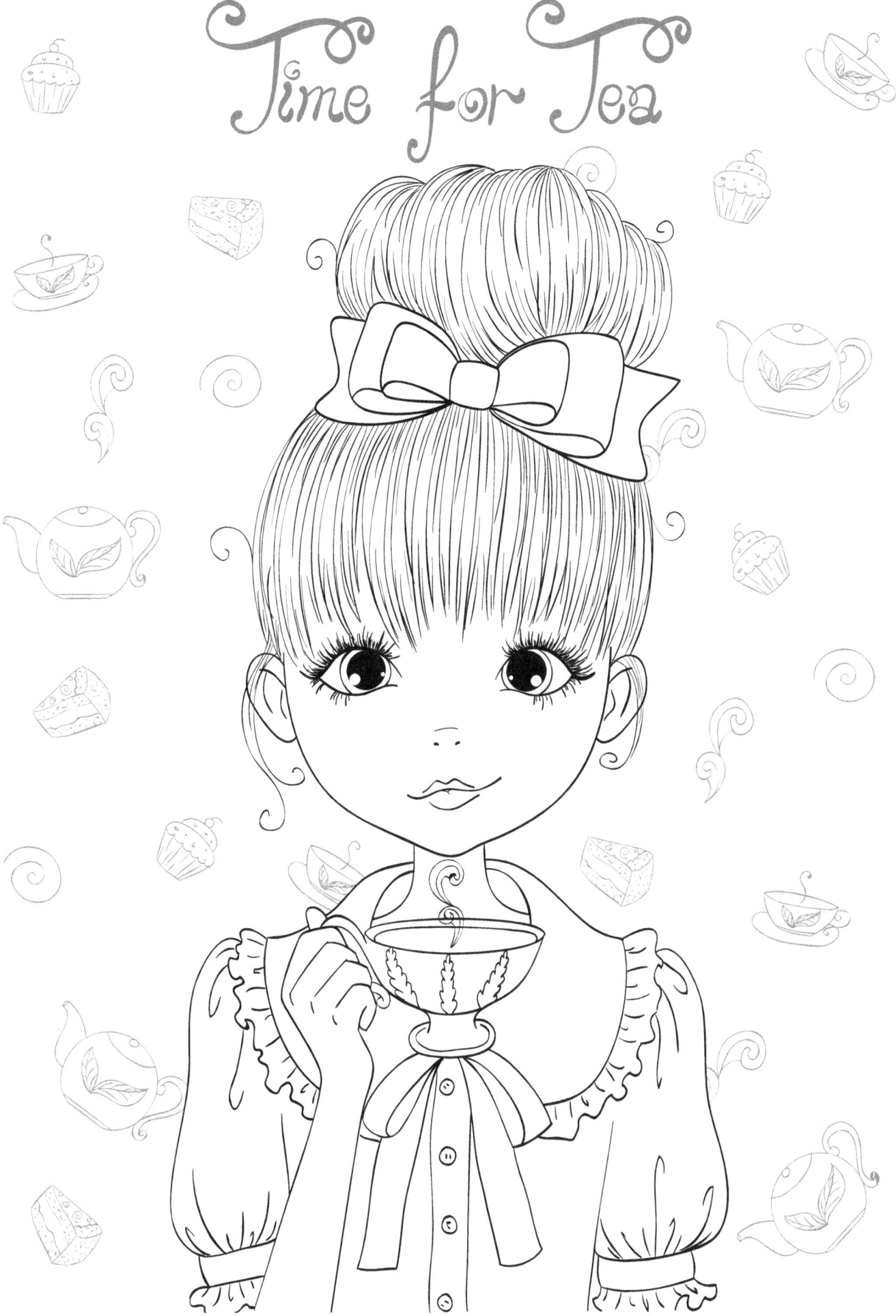

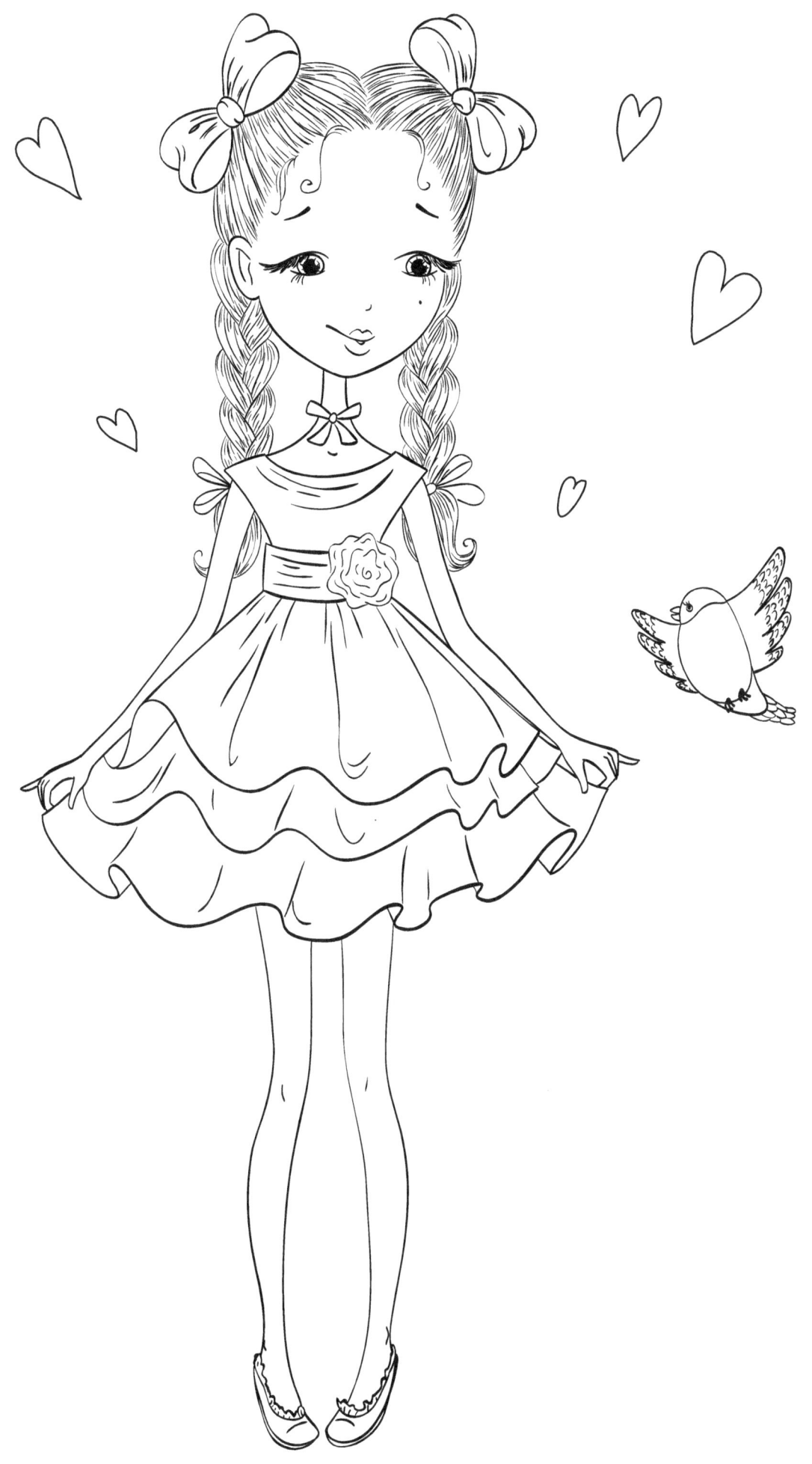

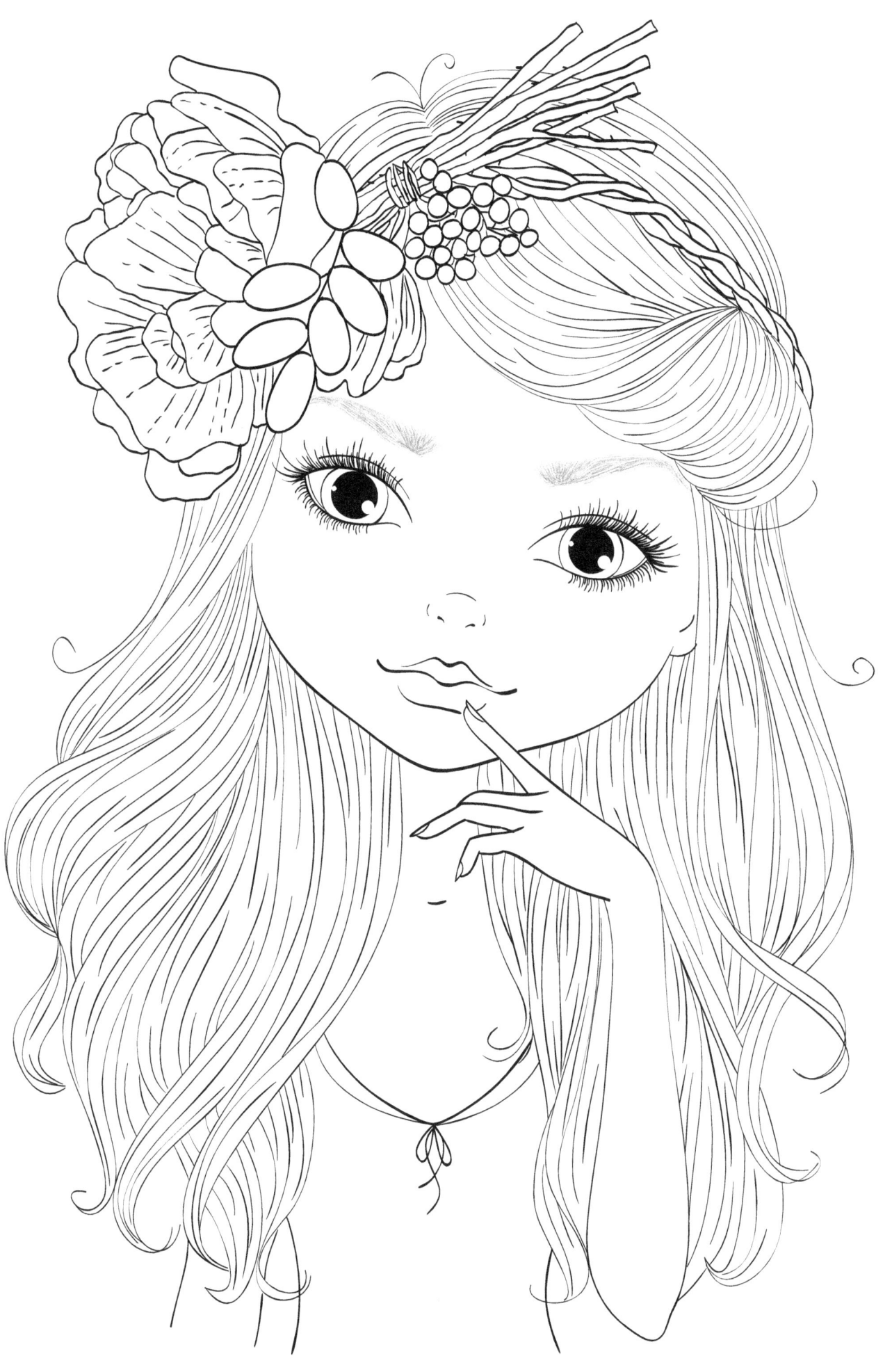

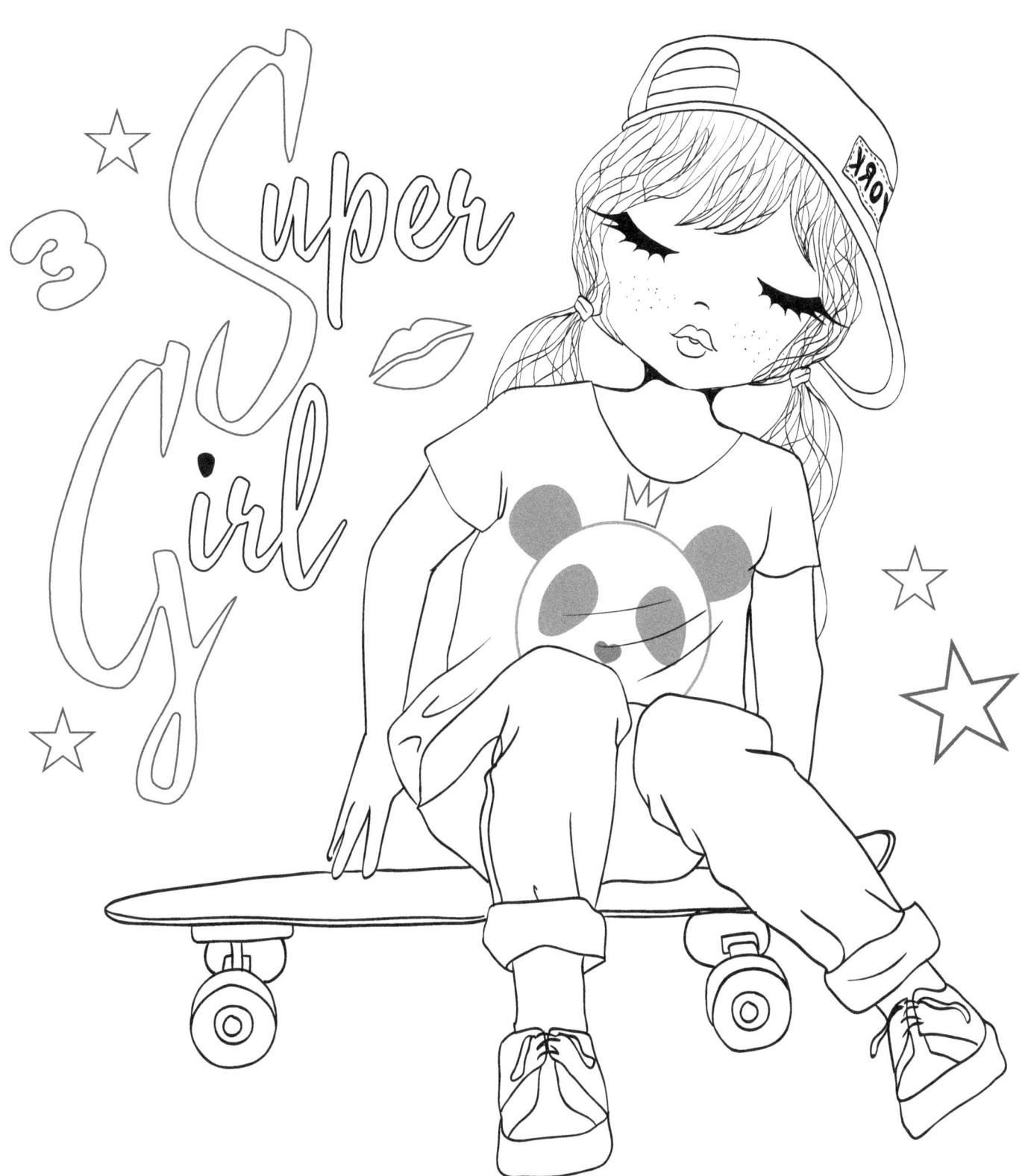

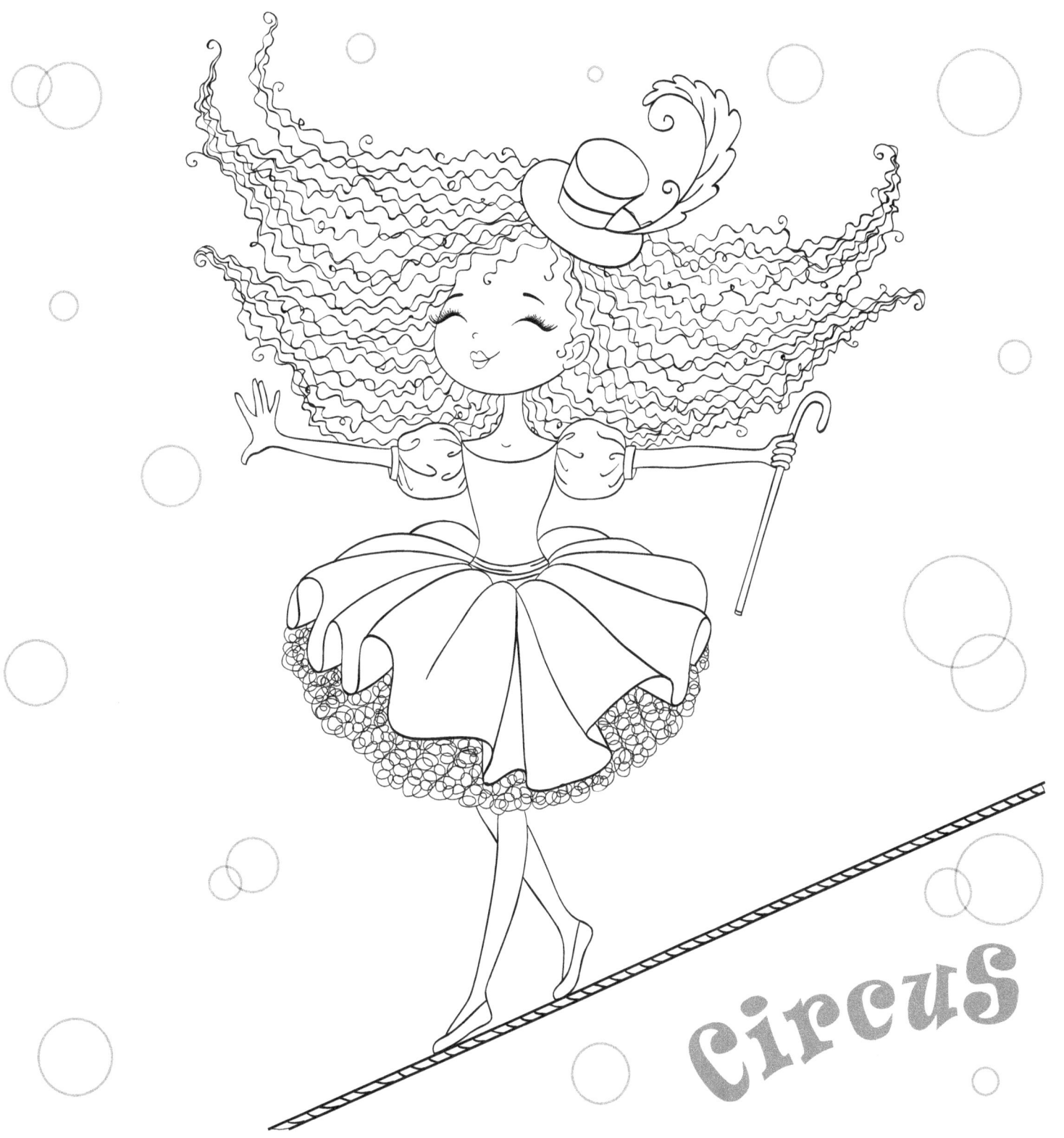

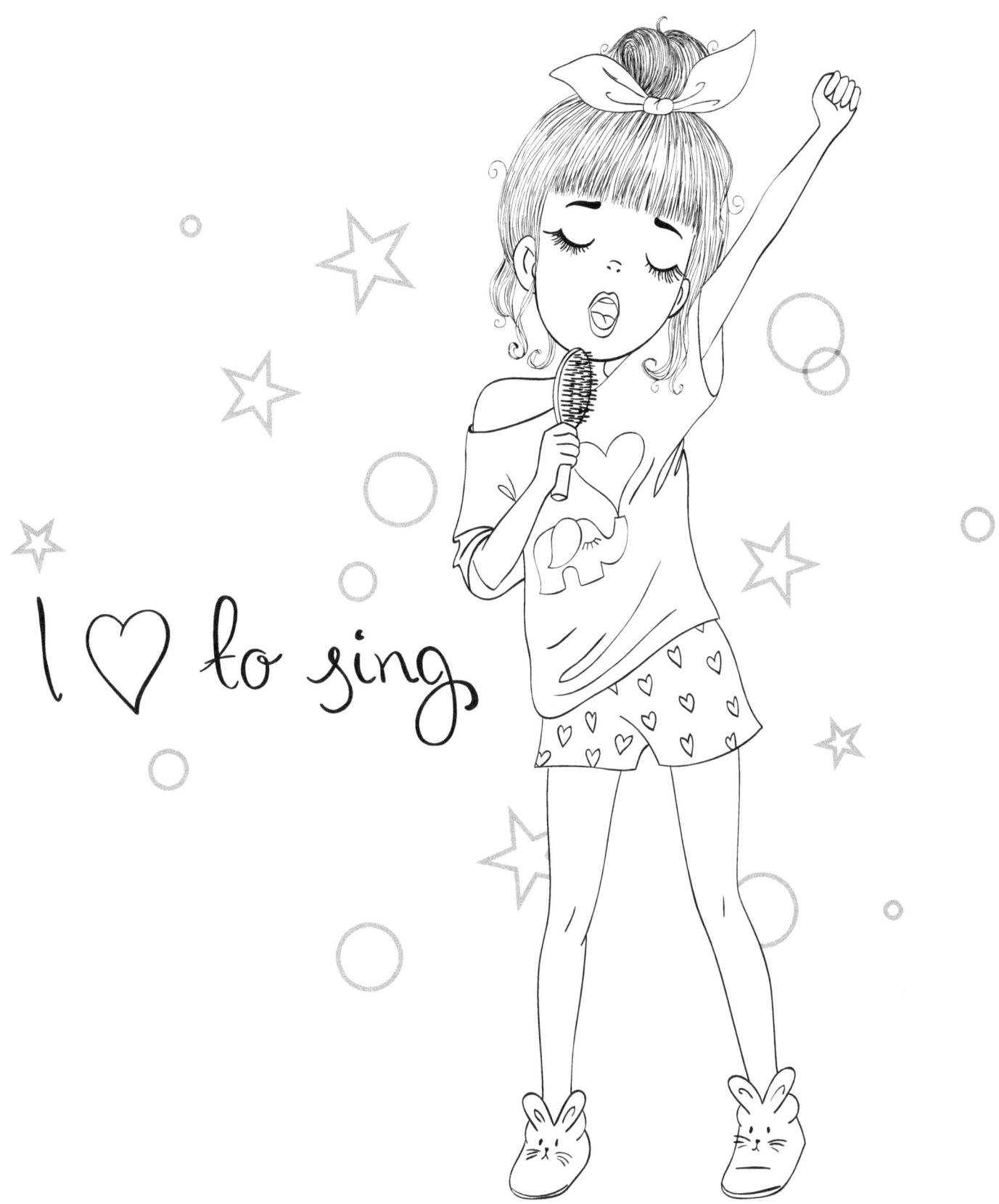

I ♥ to sing

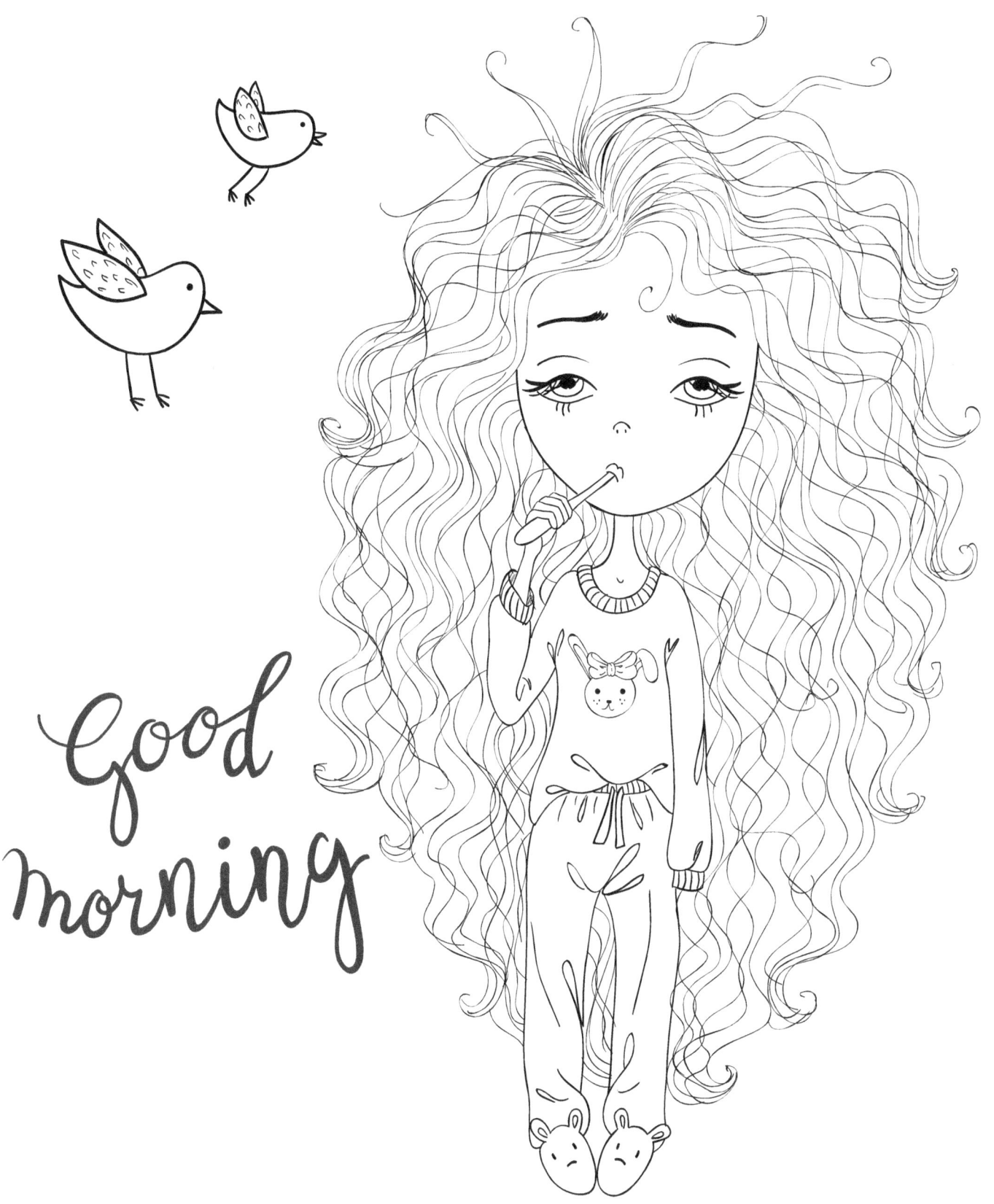

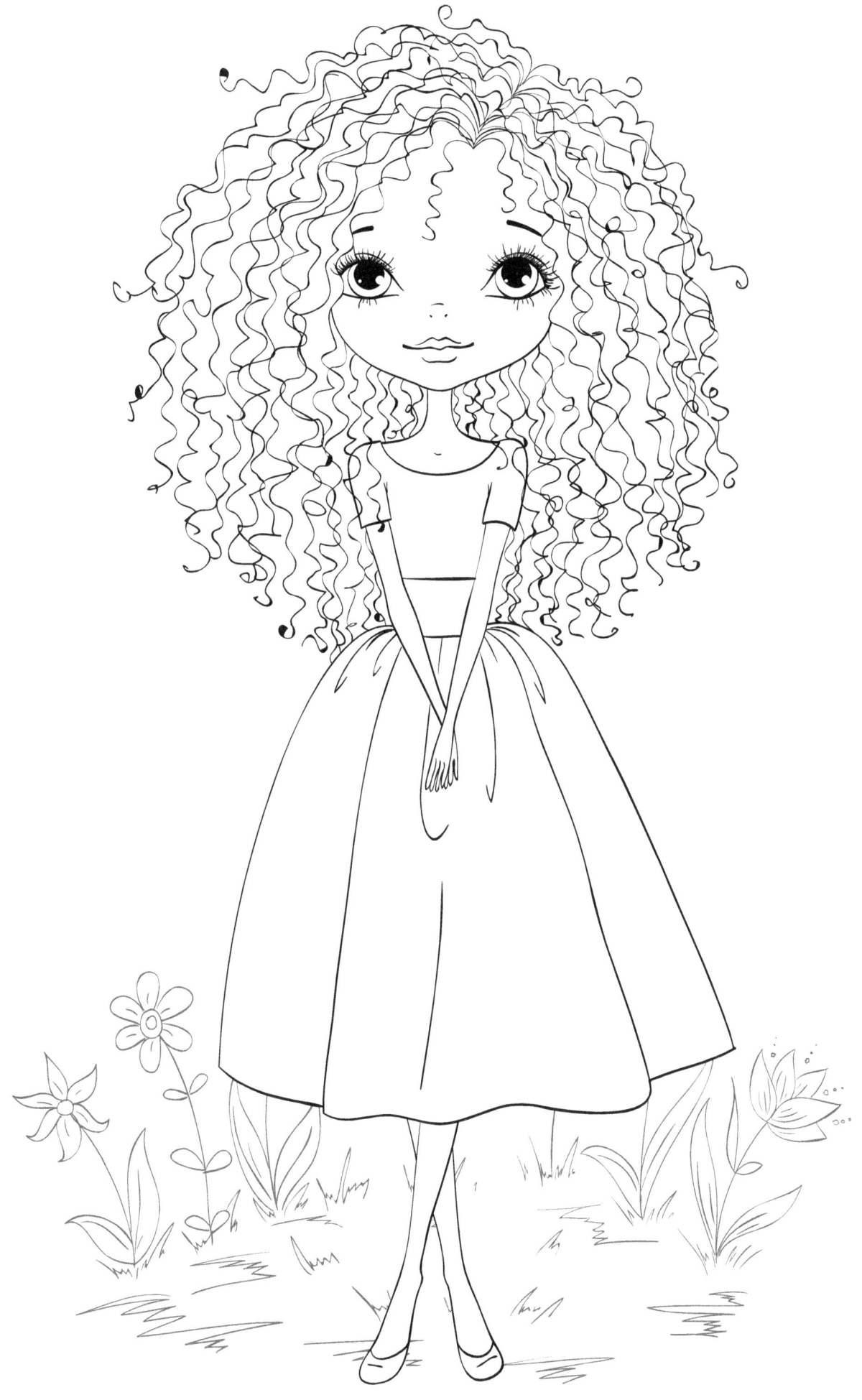

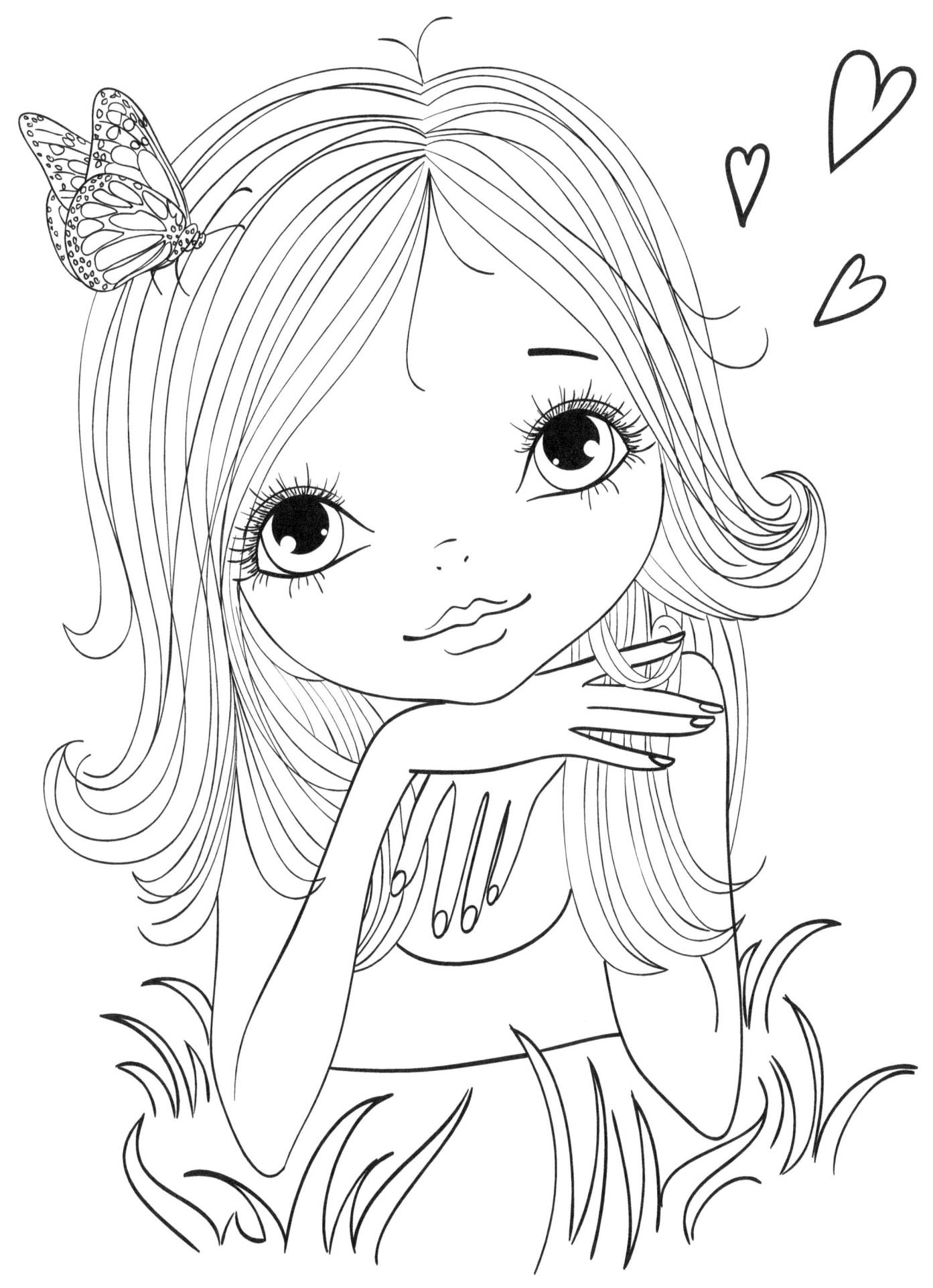

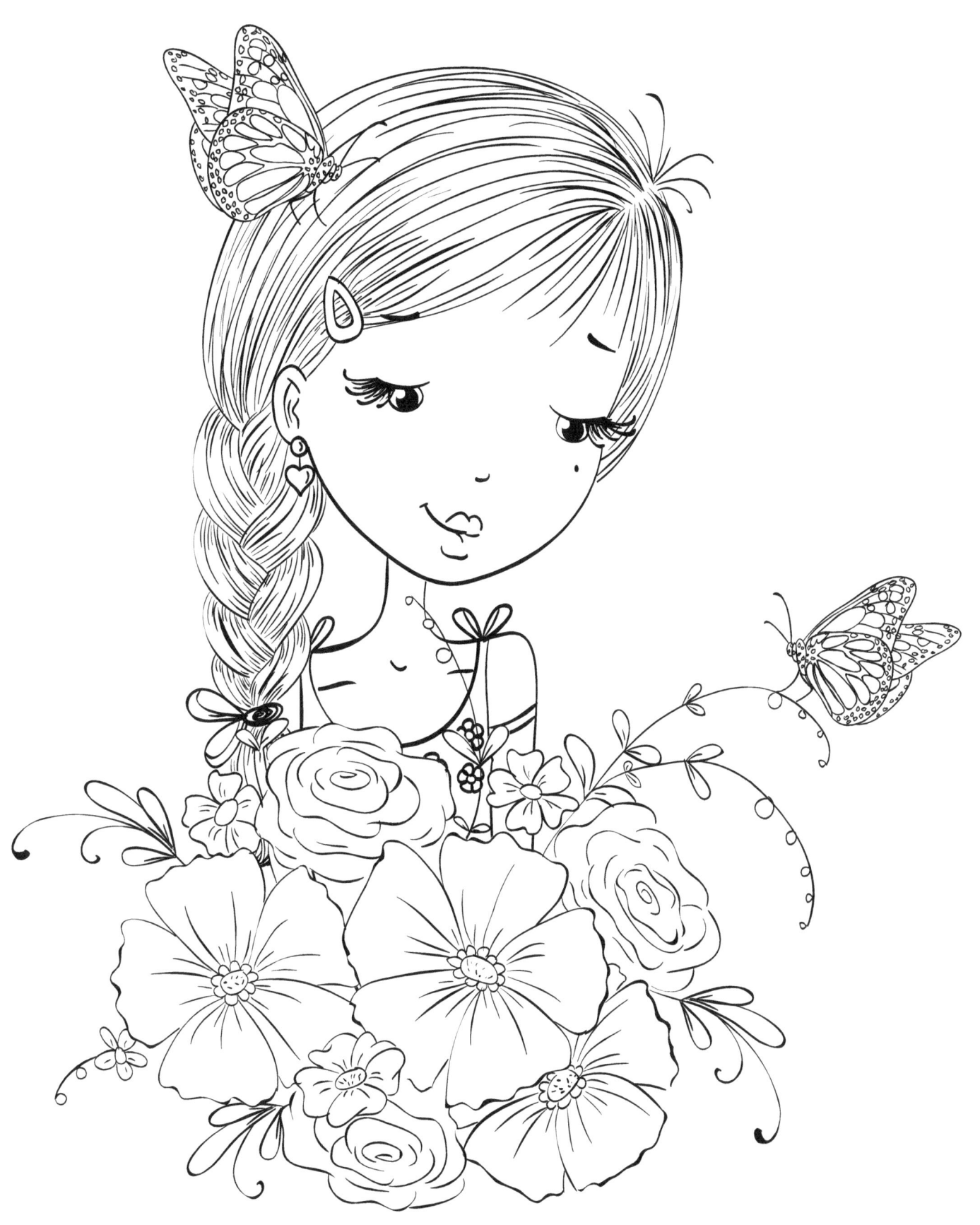

I ♥ my best friends

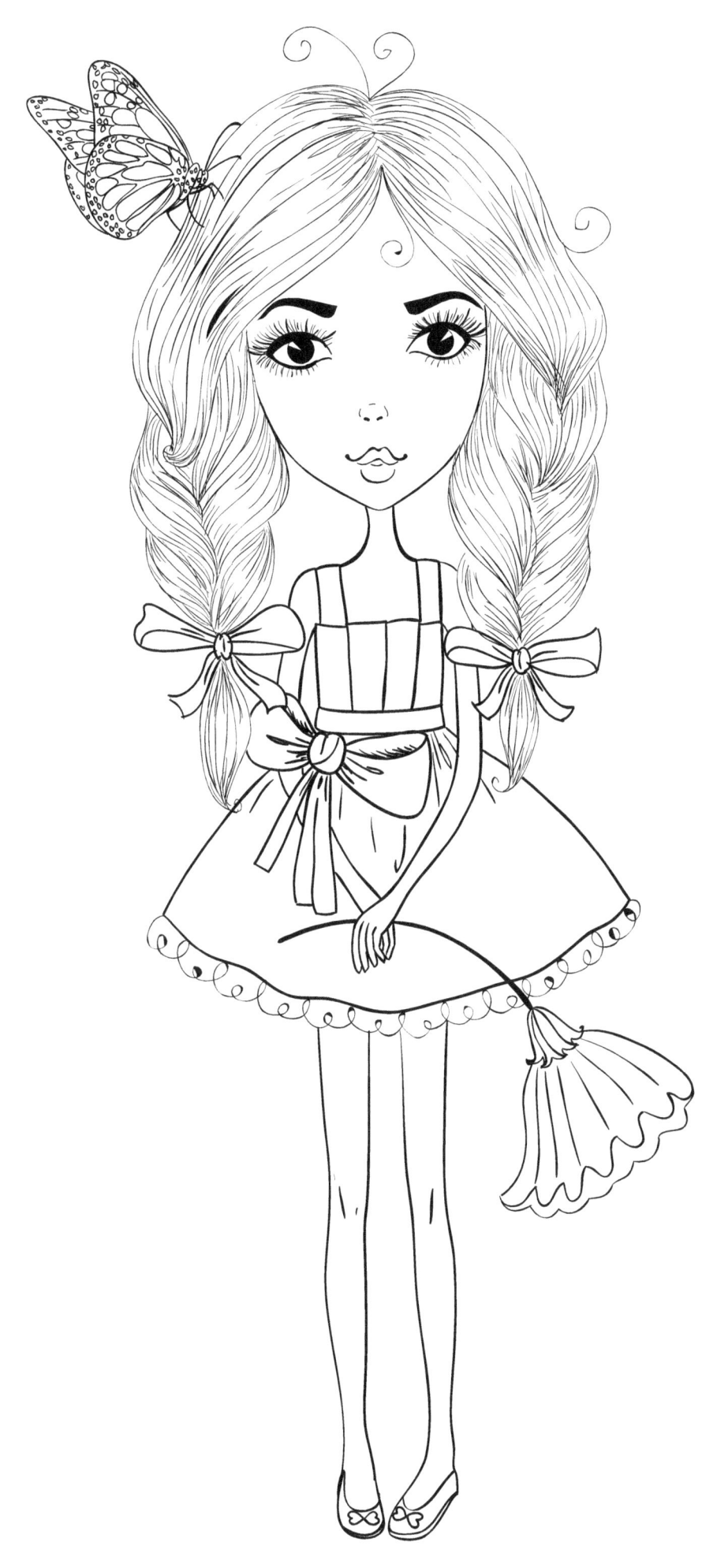

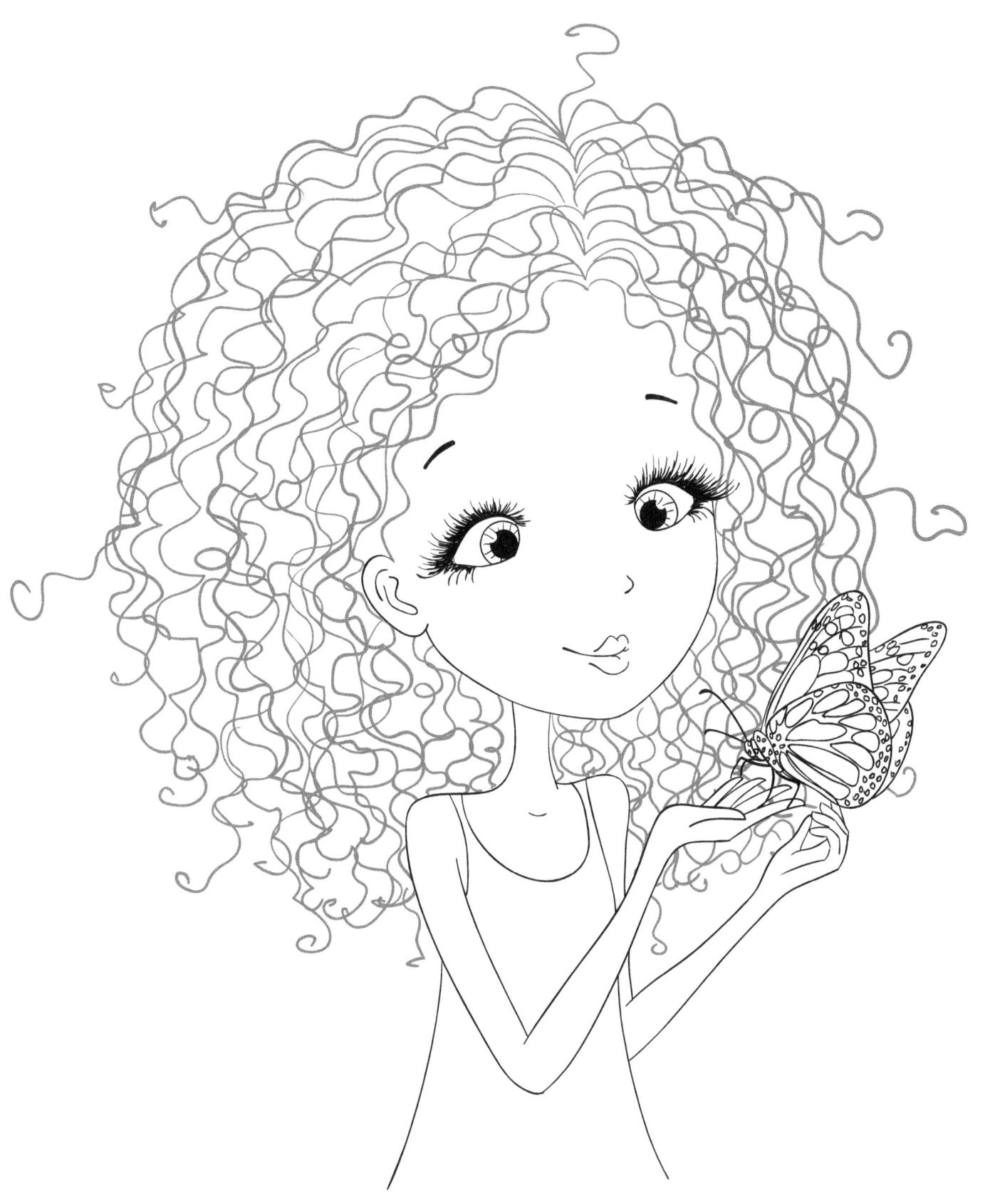

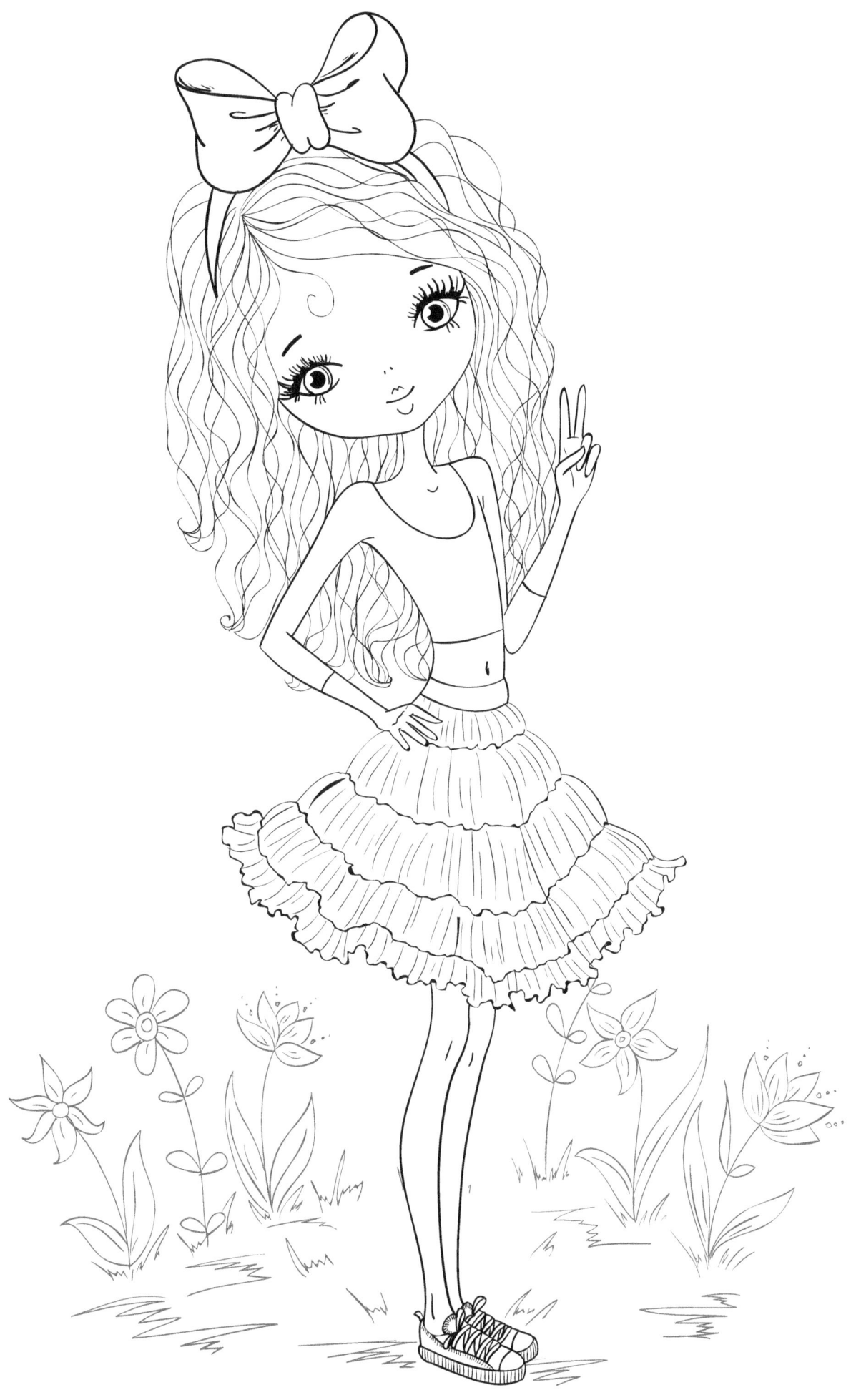

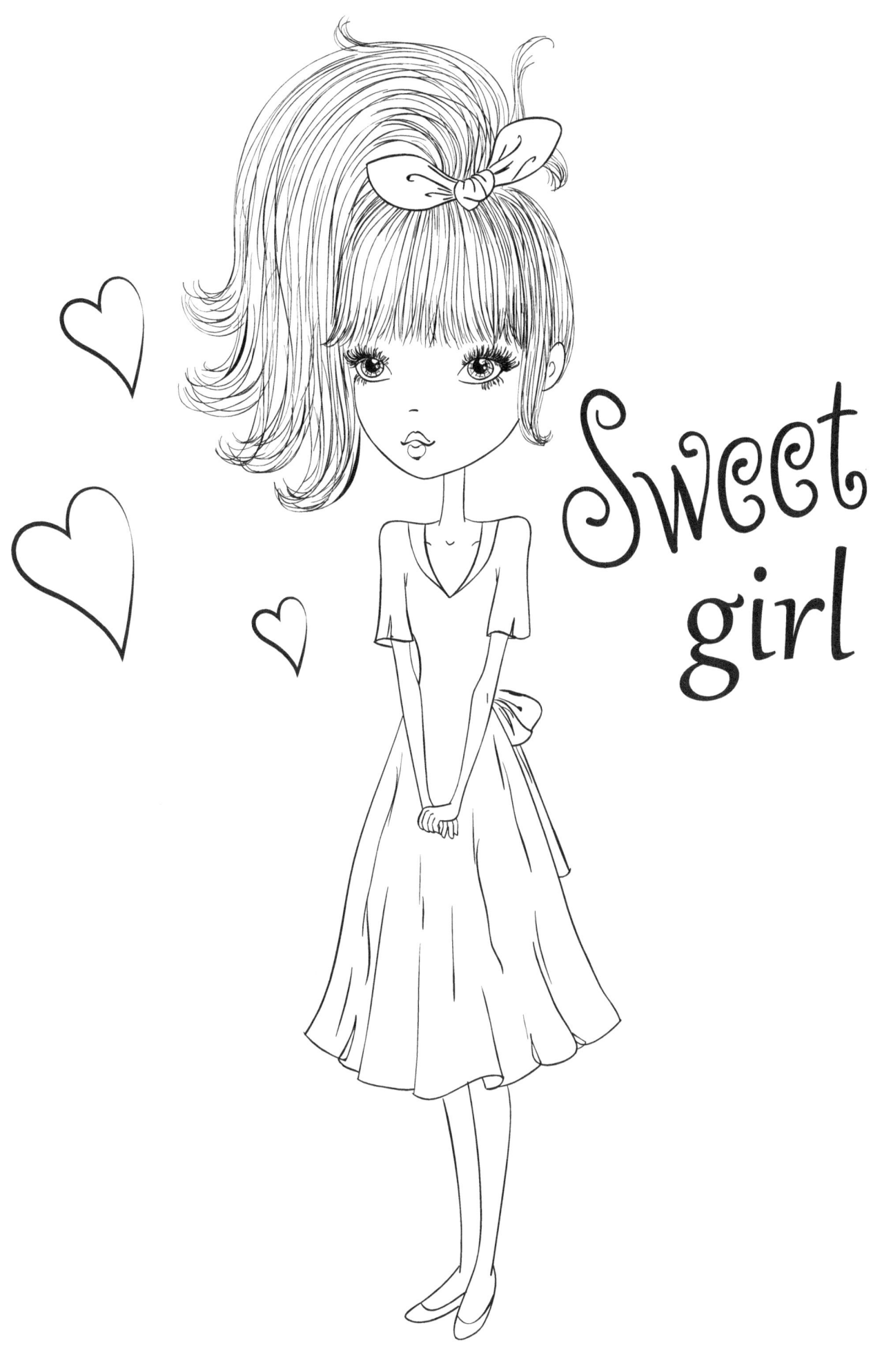

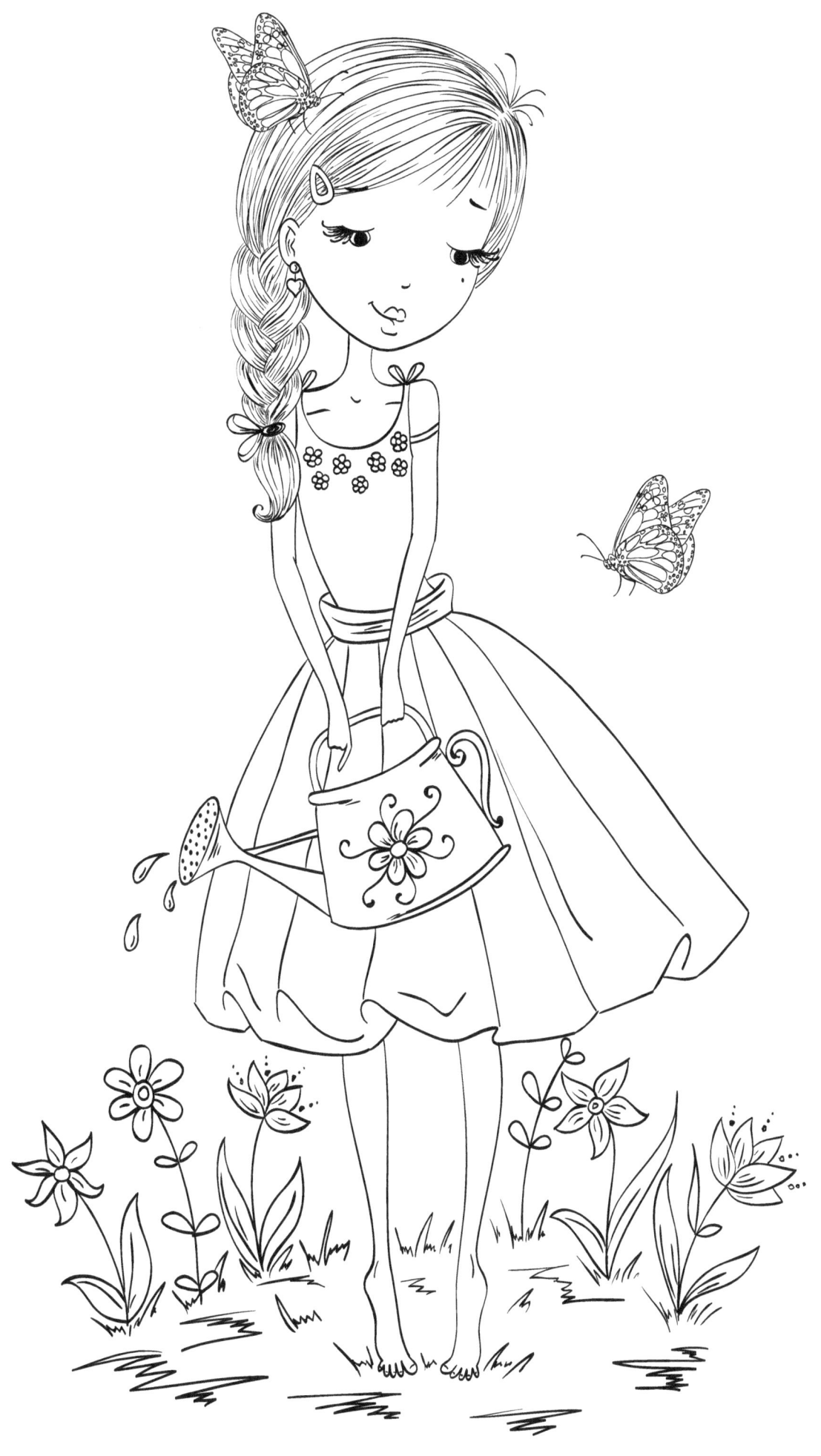

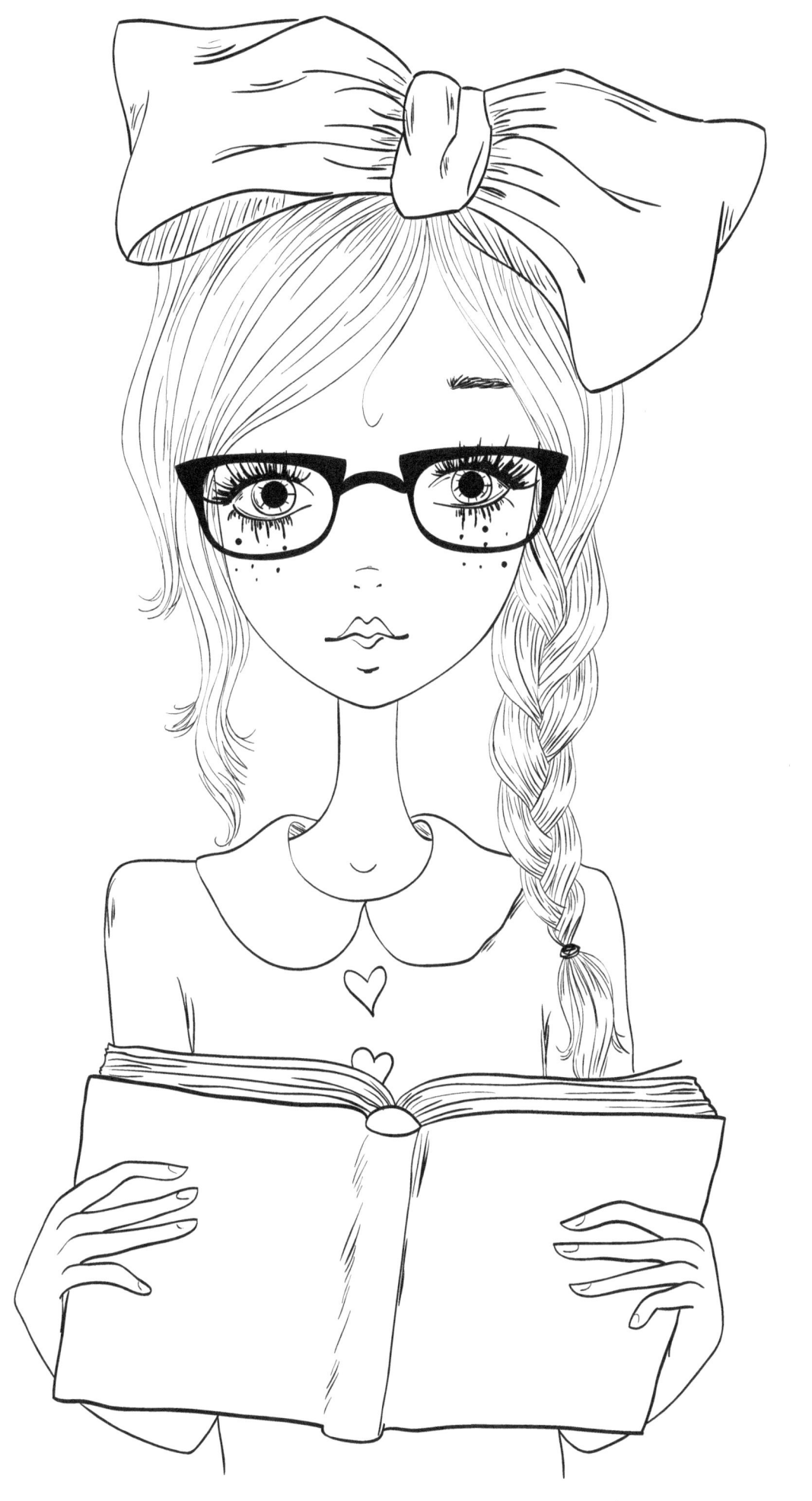

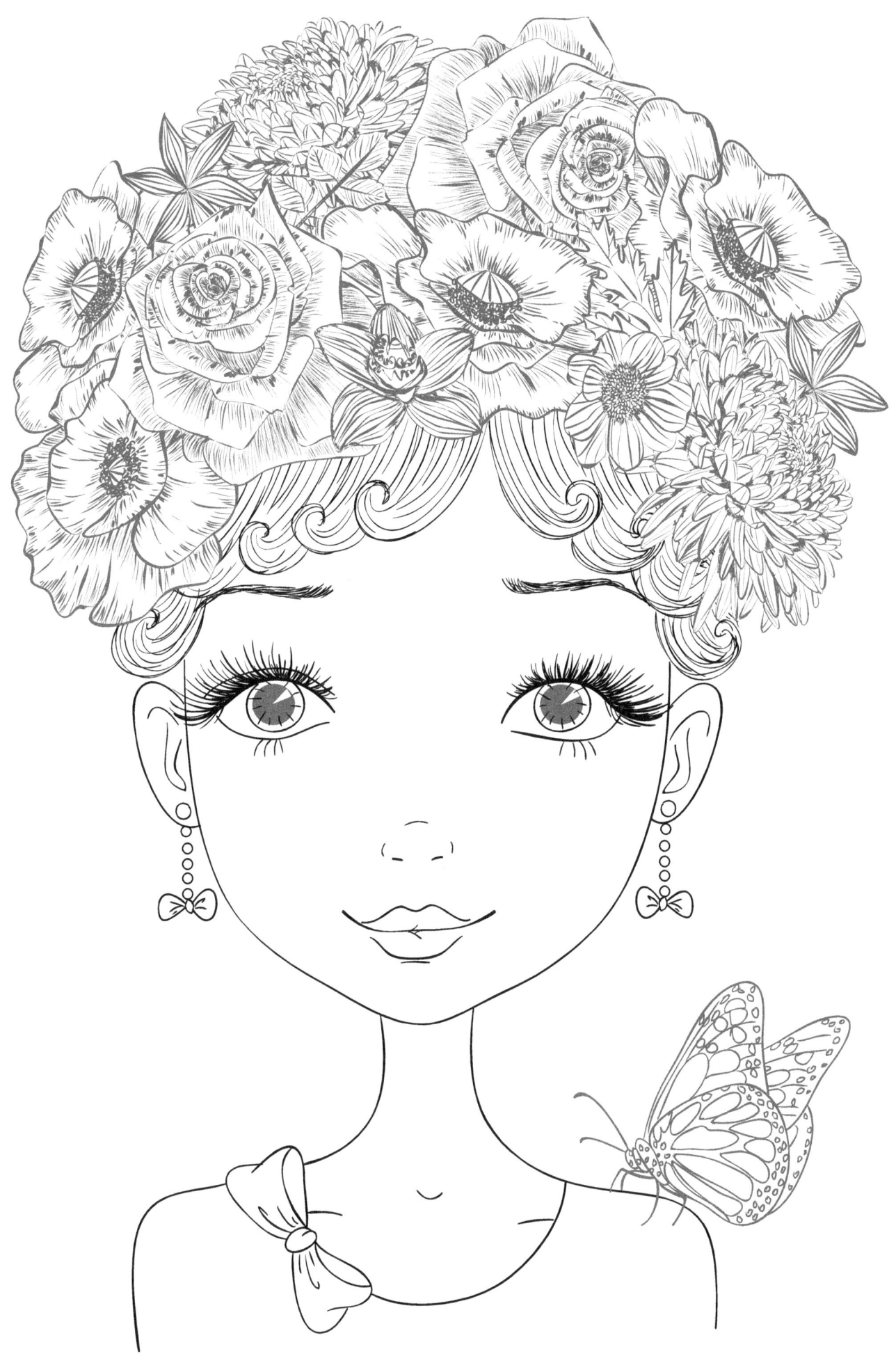

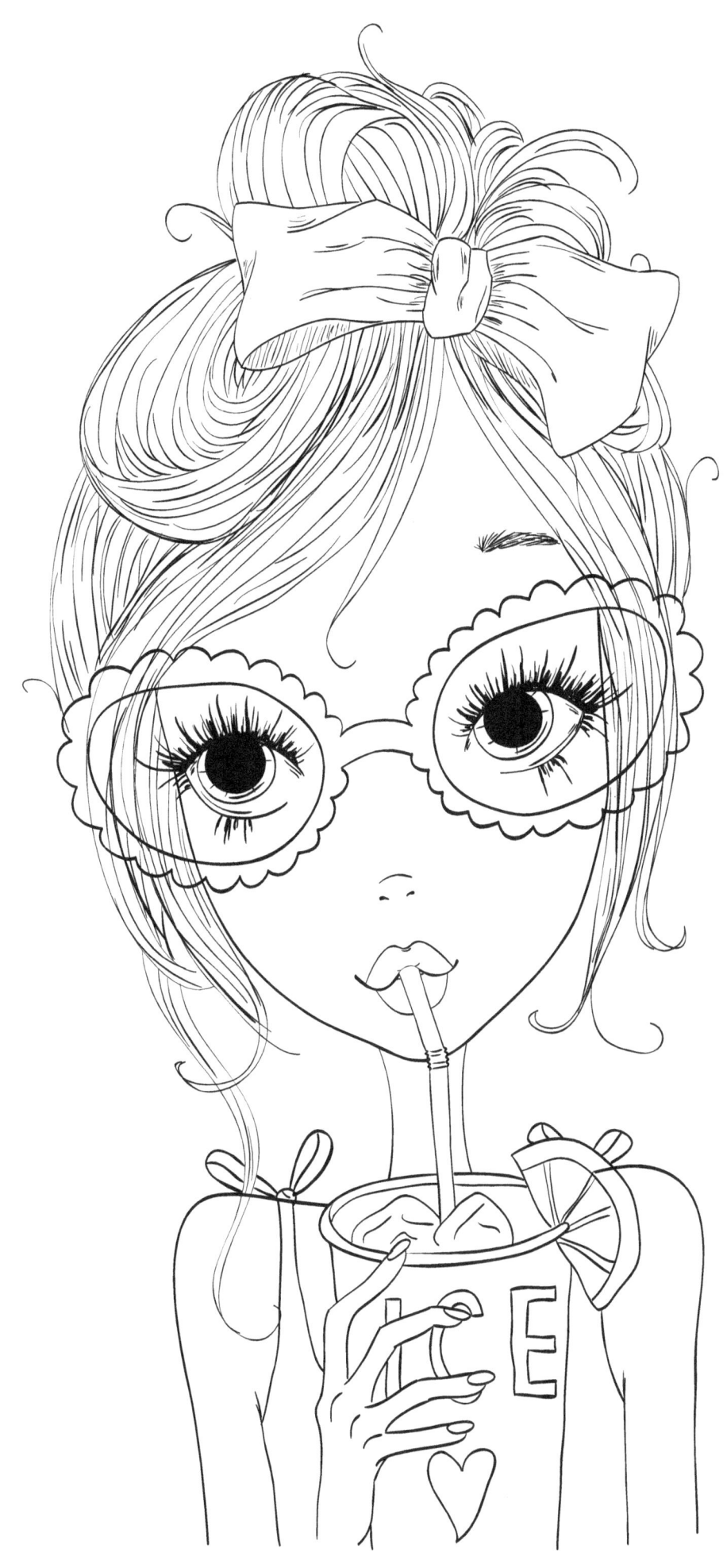

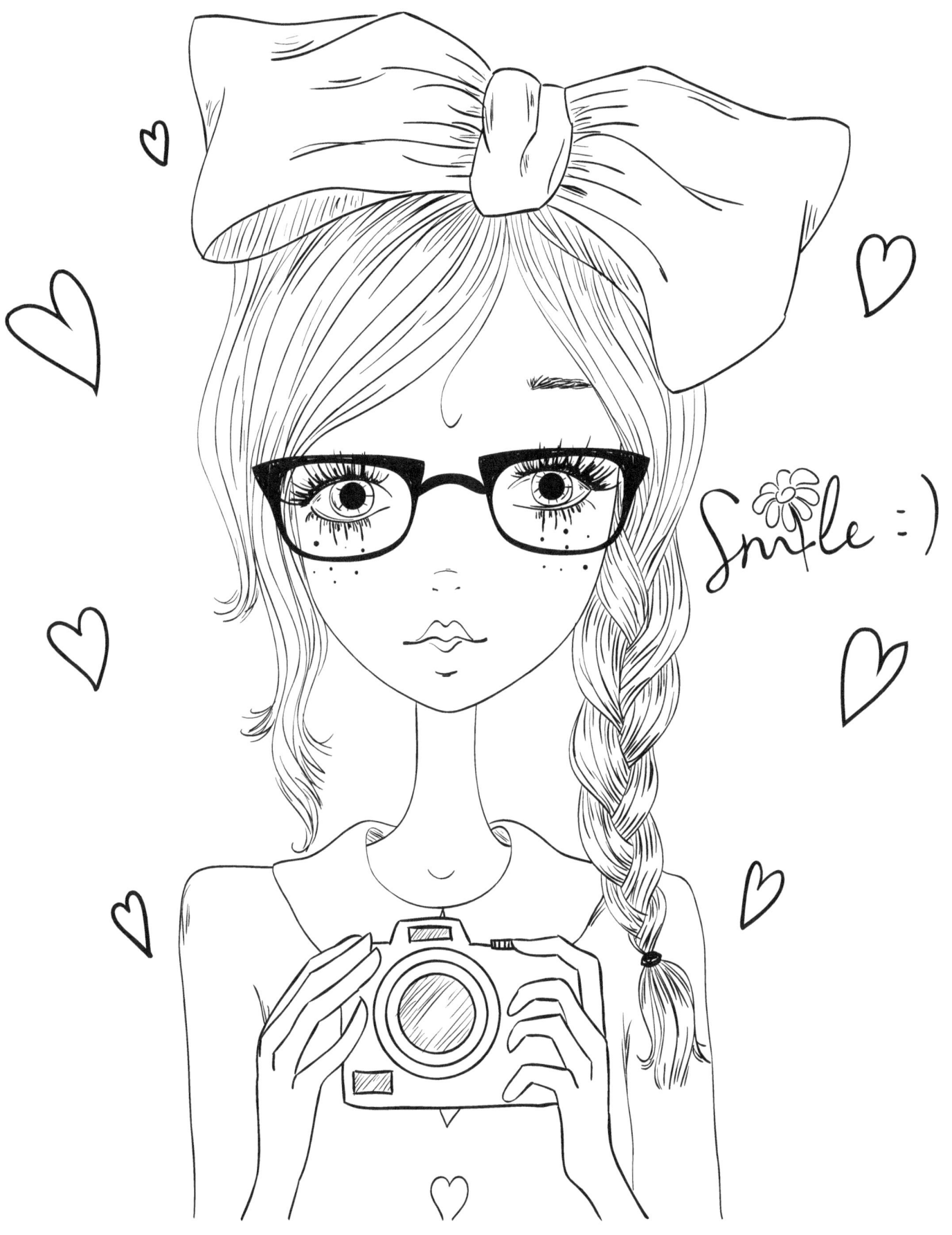

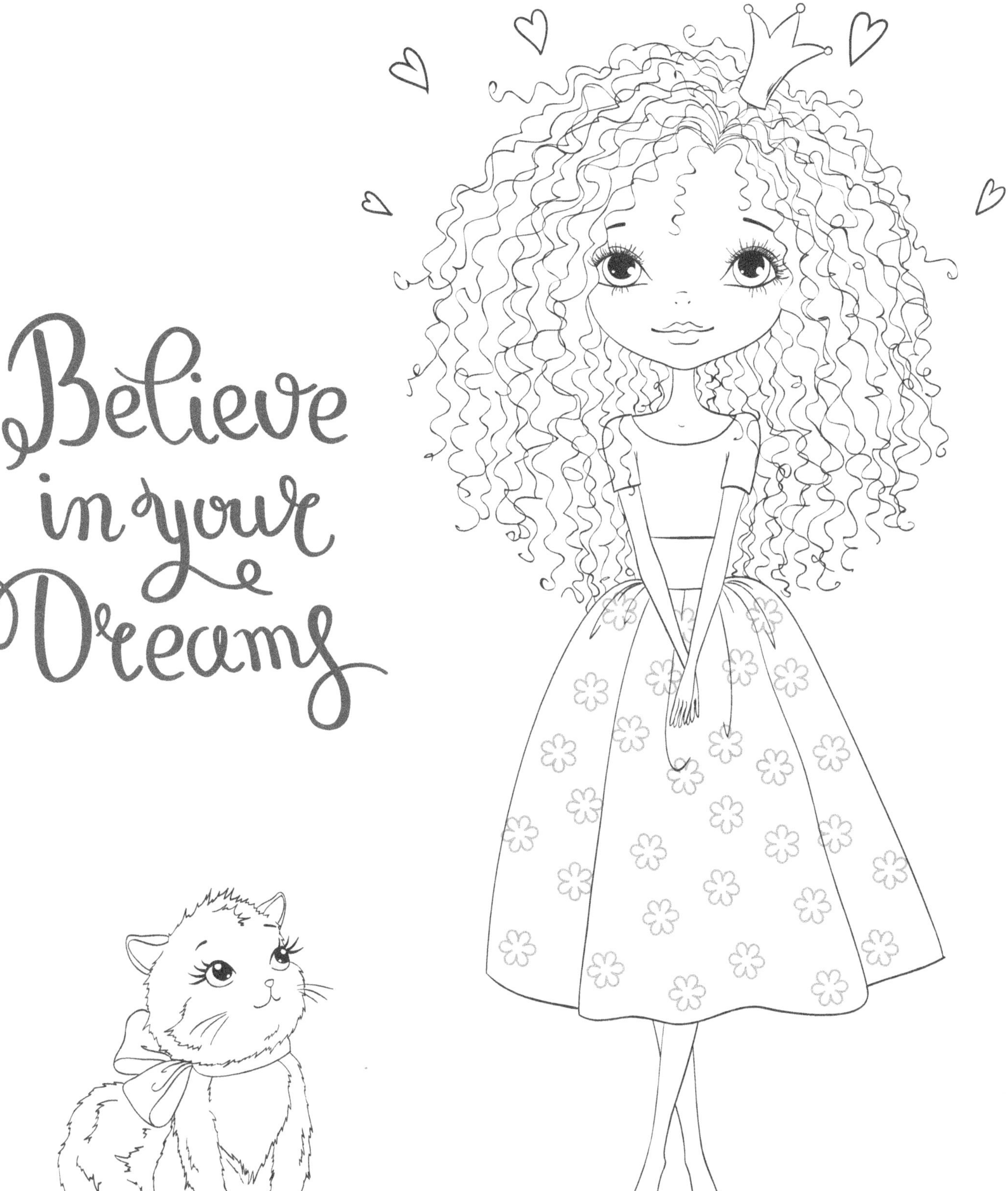

Believe
in your
Dreams

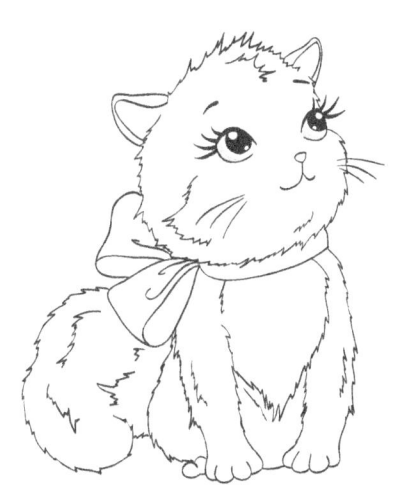

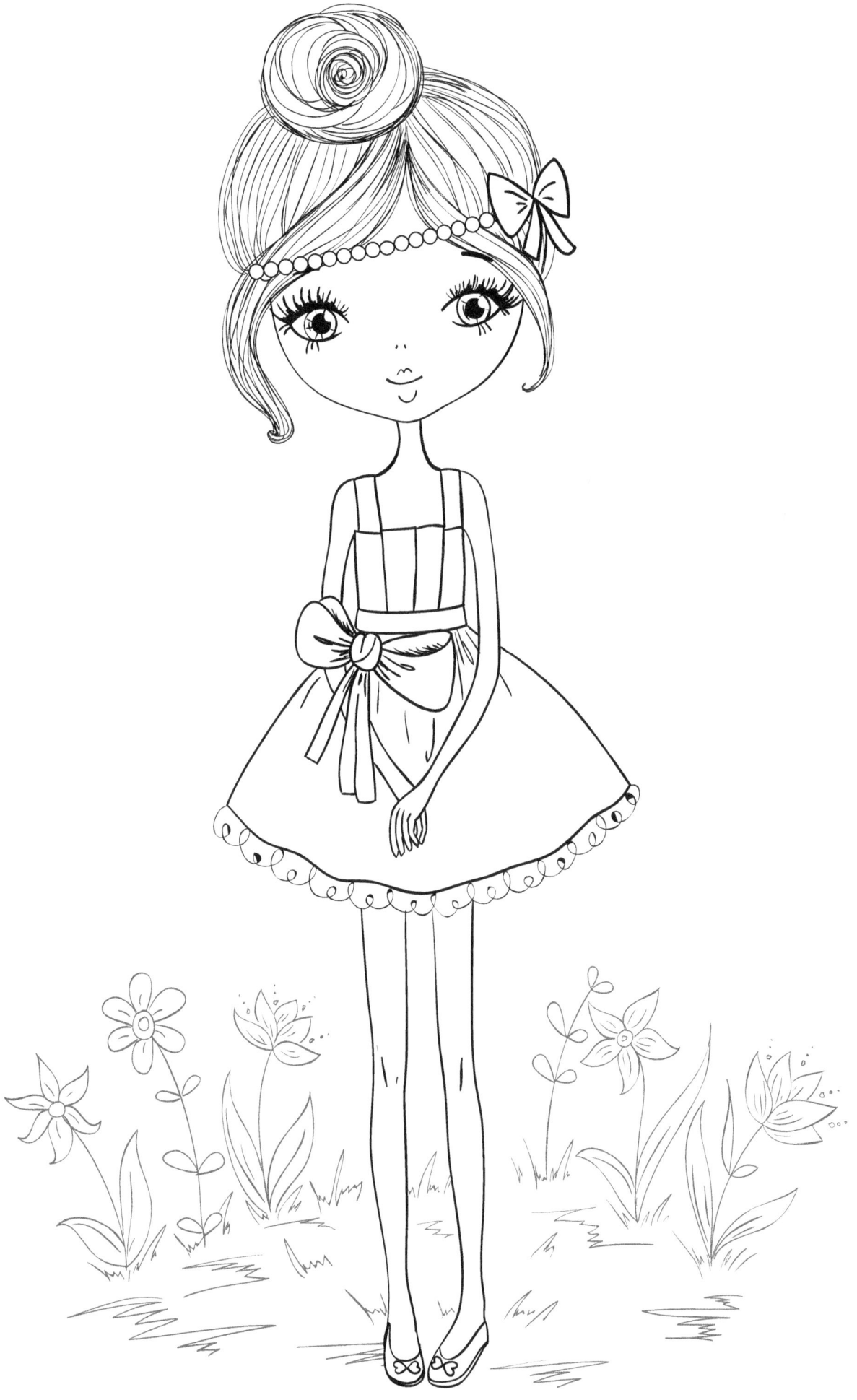

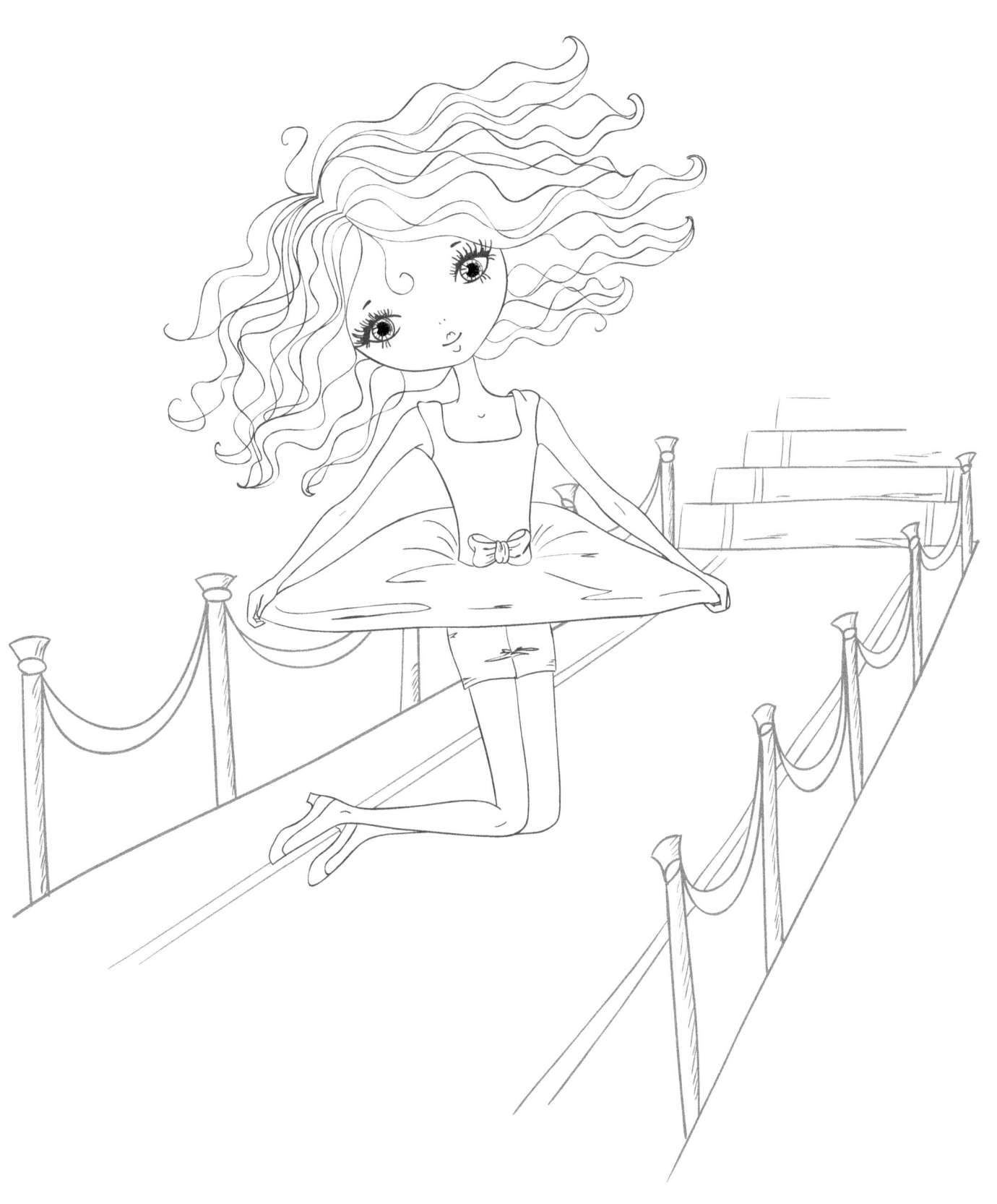

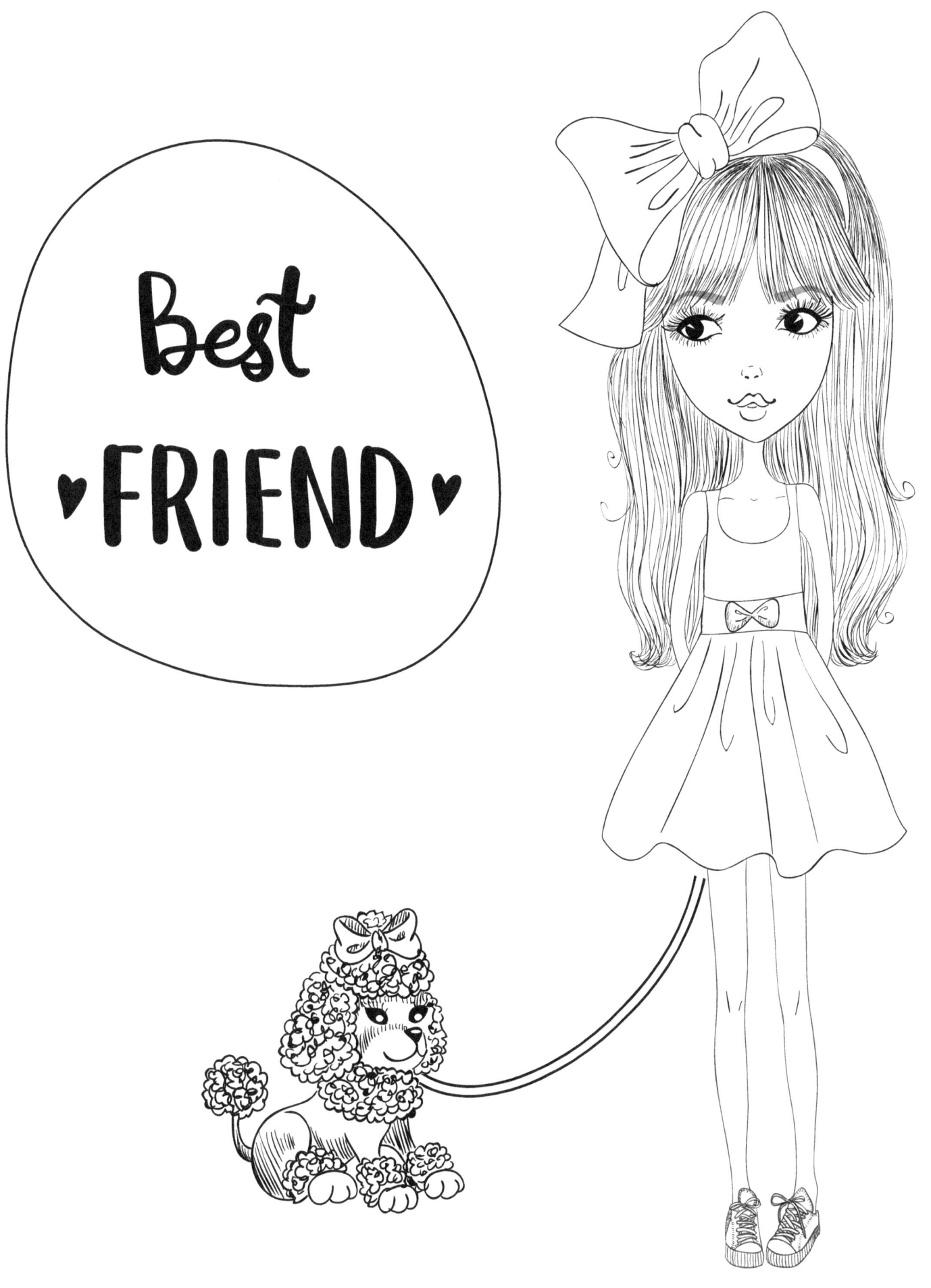

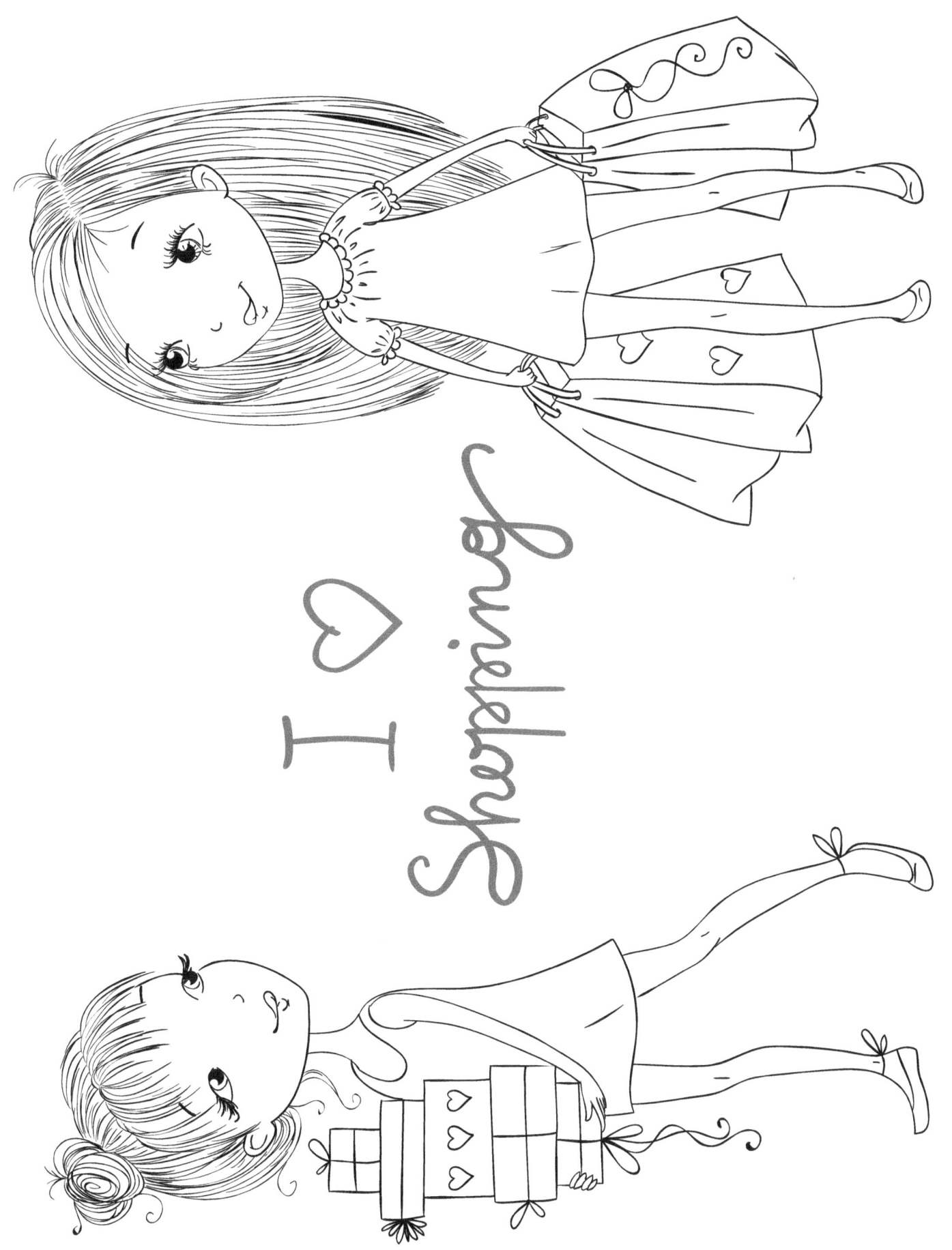

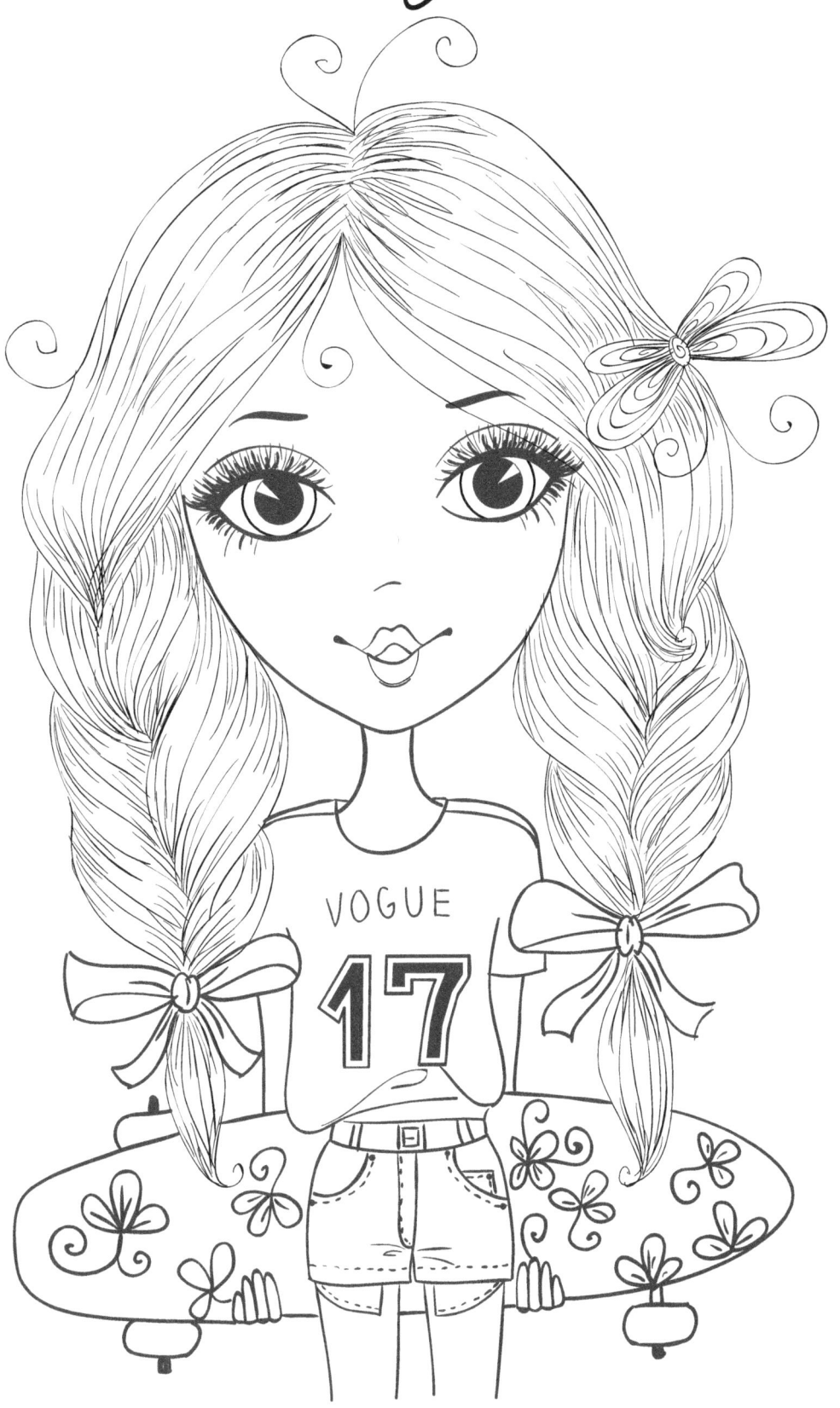

Let's go Roller

Skating !

life is beautiful

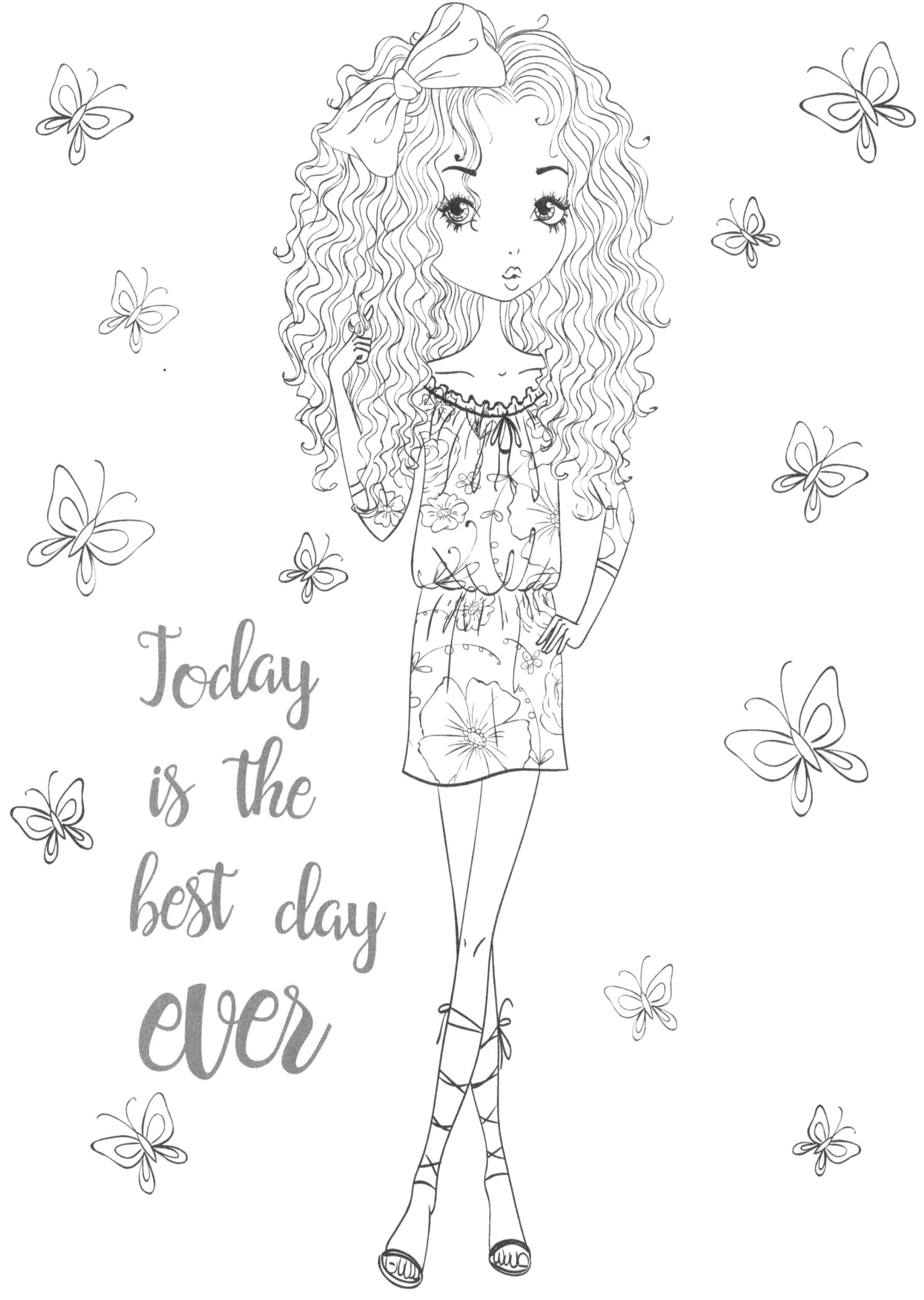

Today is the best day ever

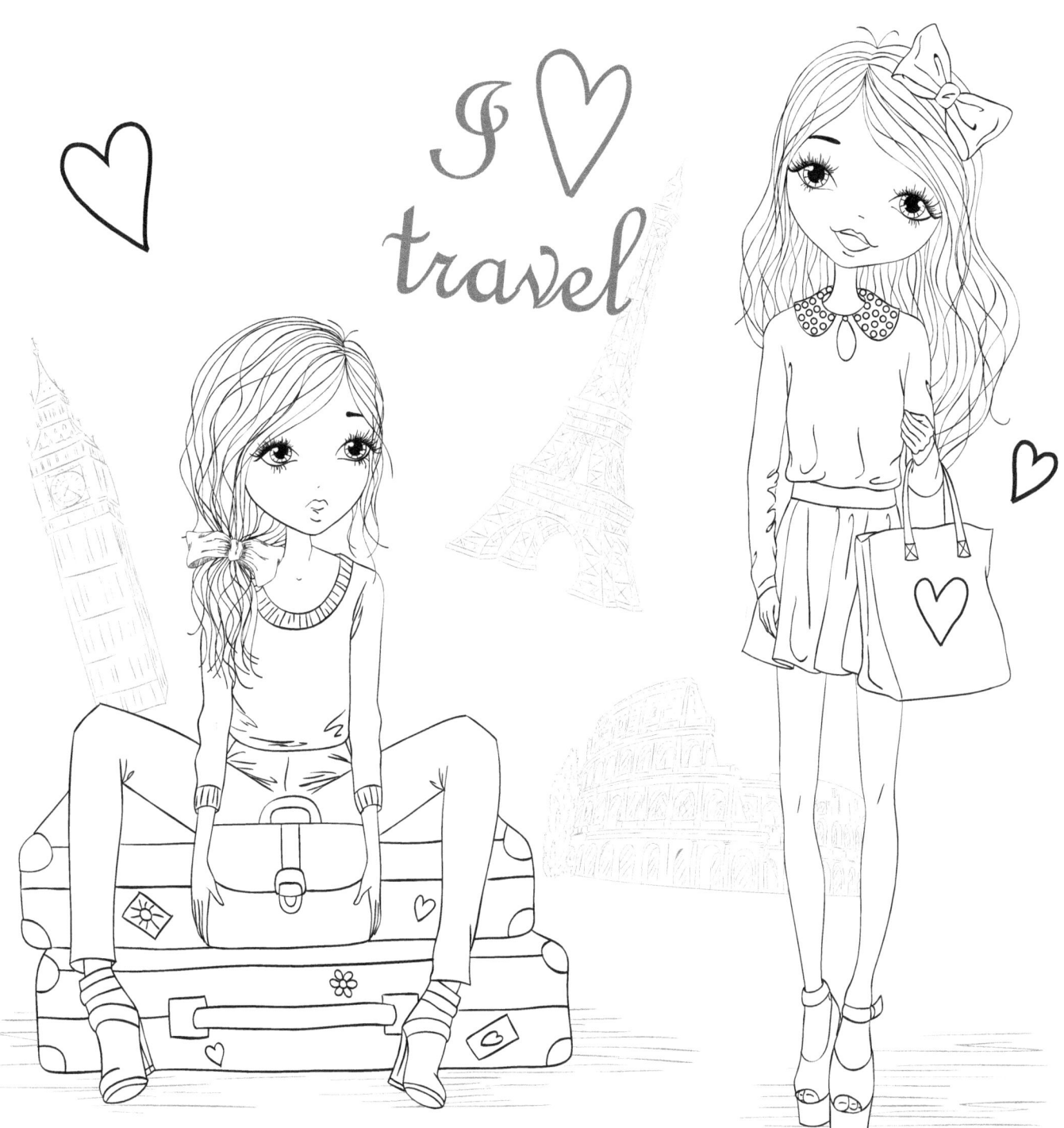

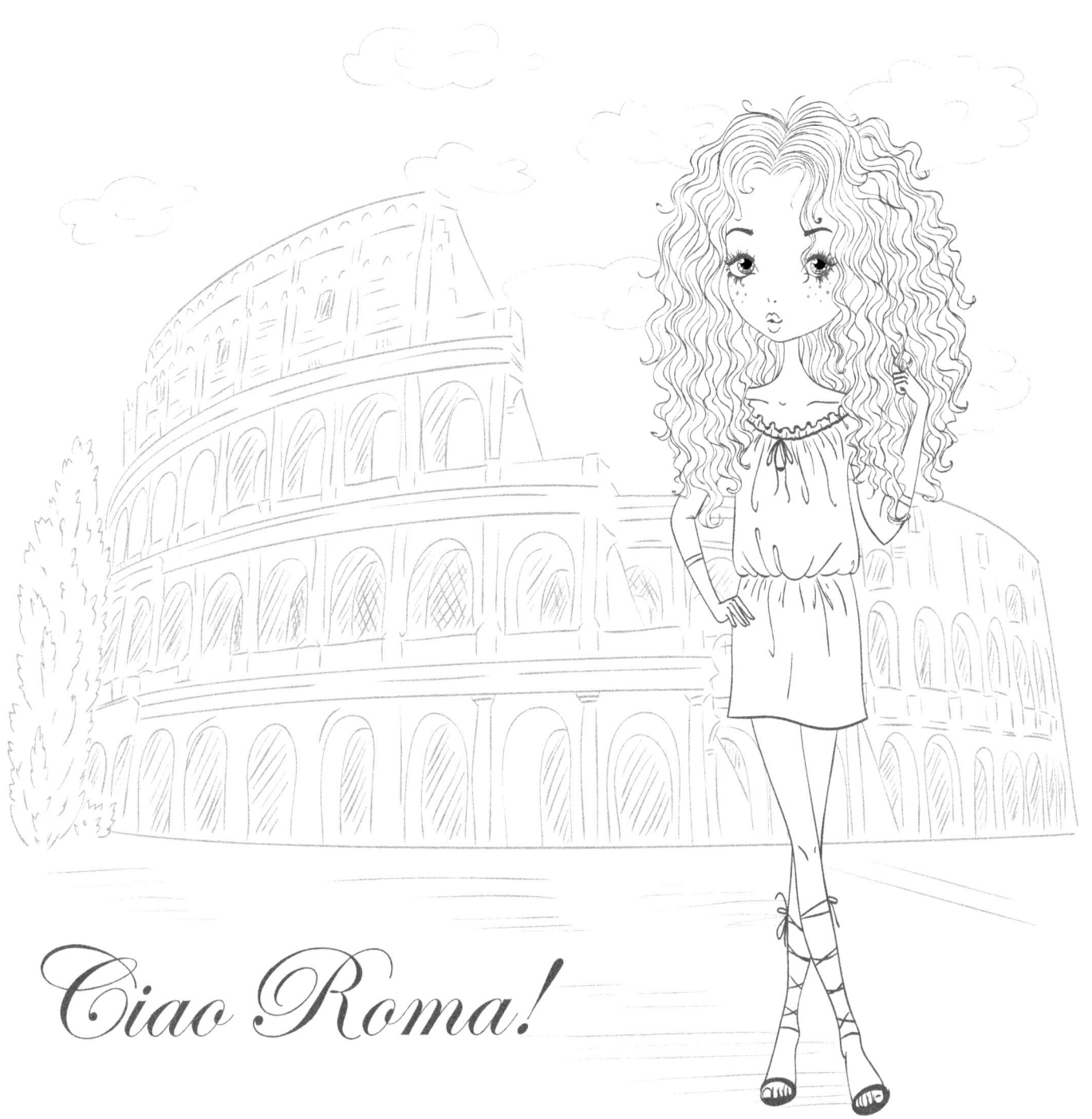

Ciao Roma!

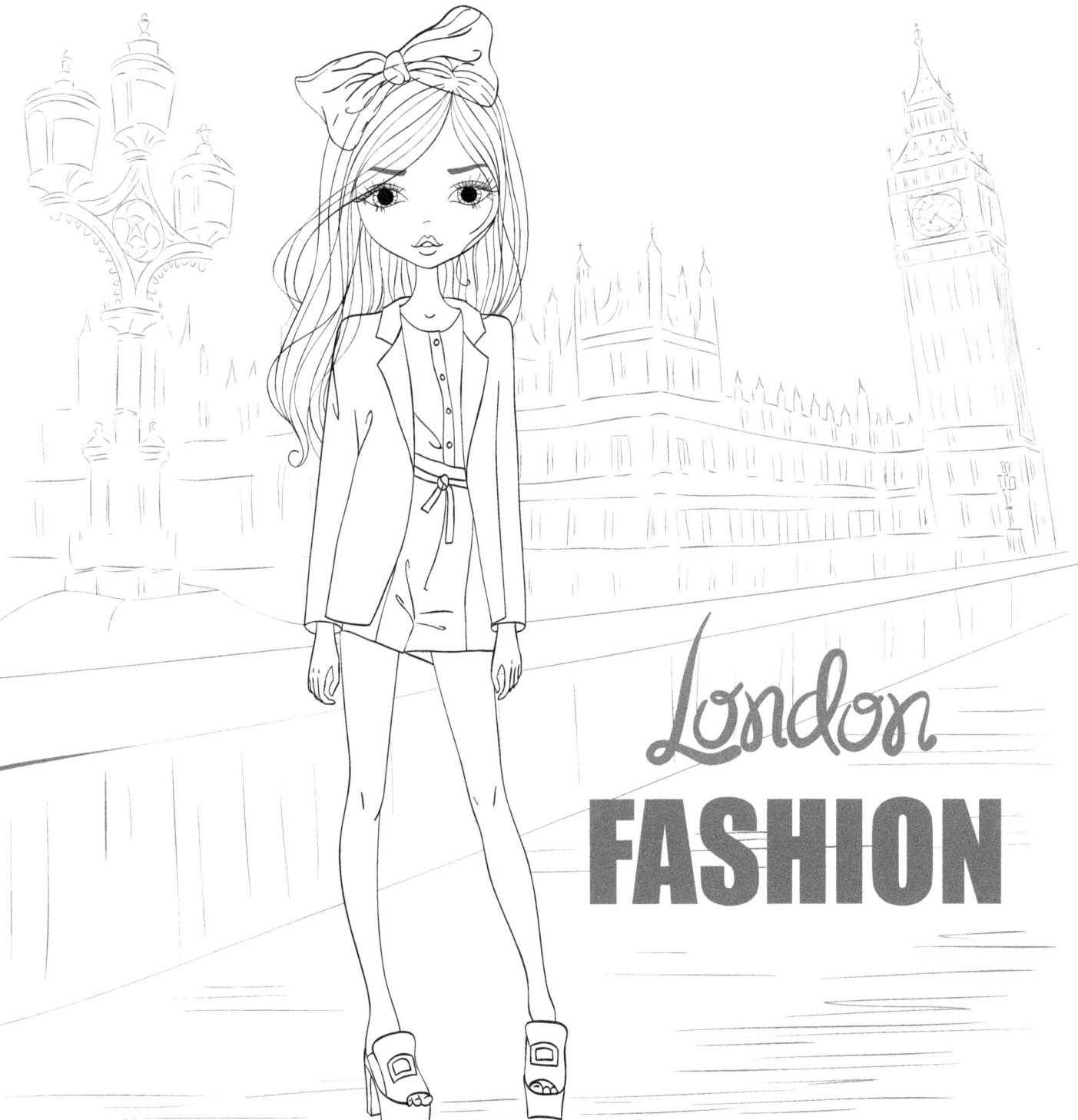

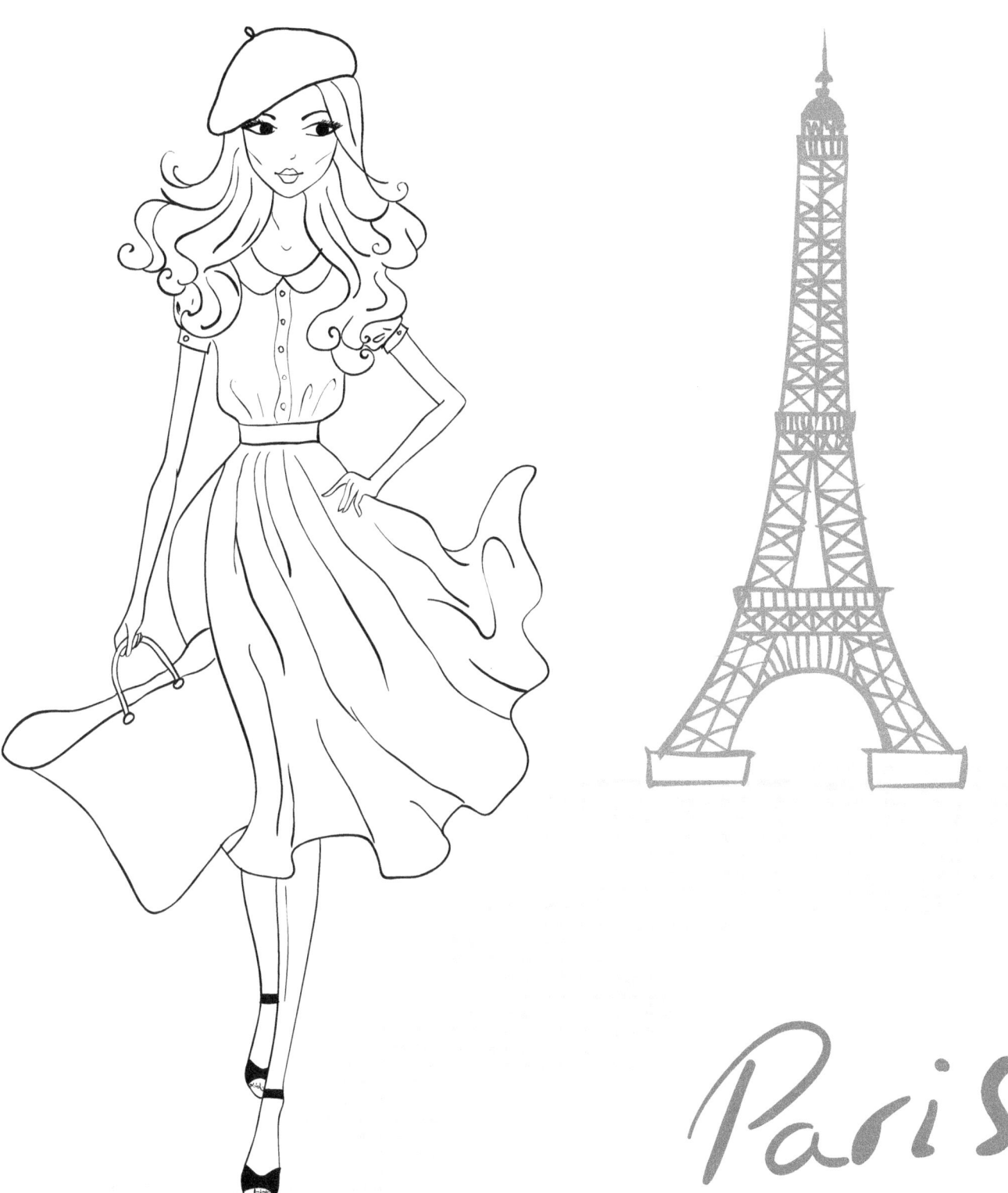

Paris

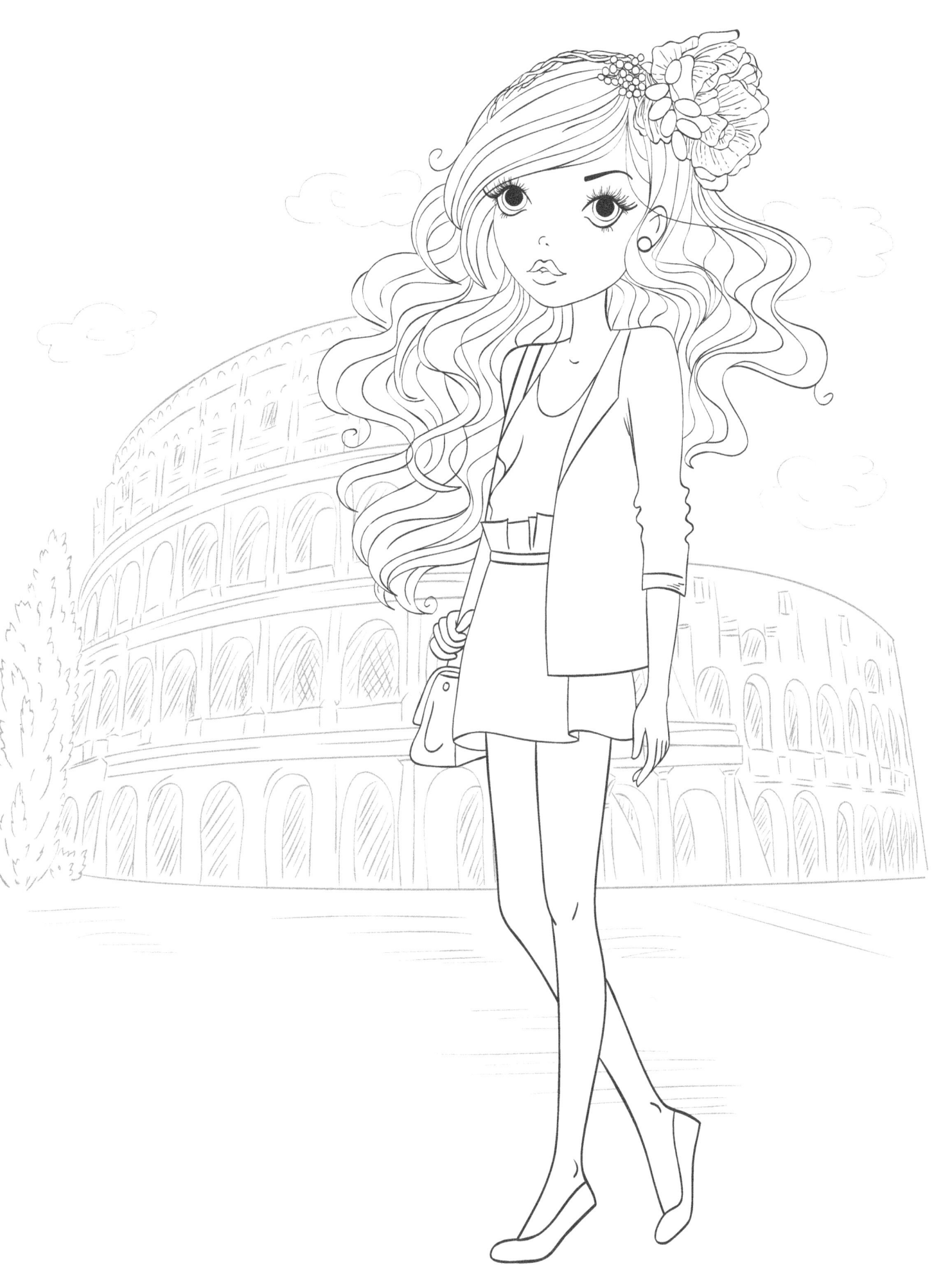

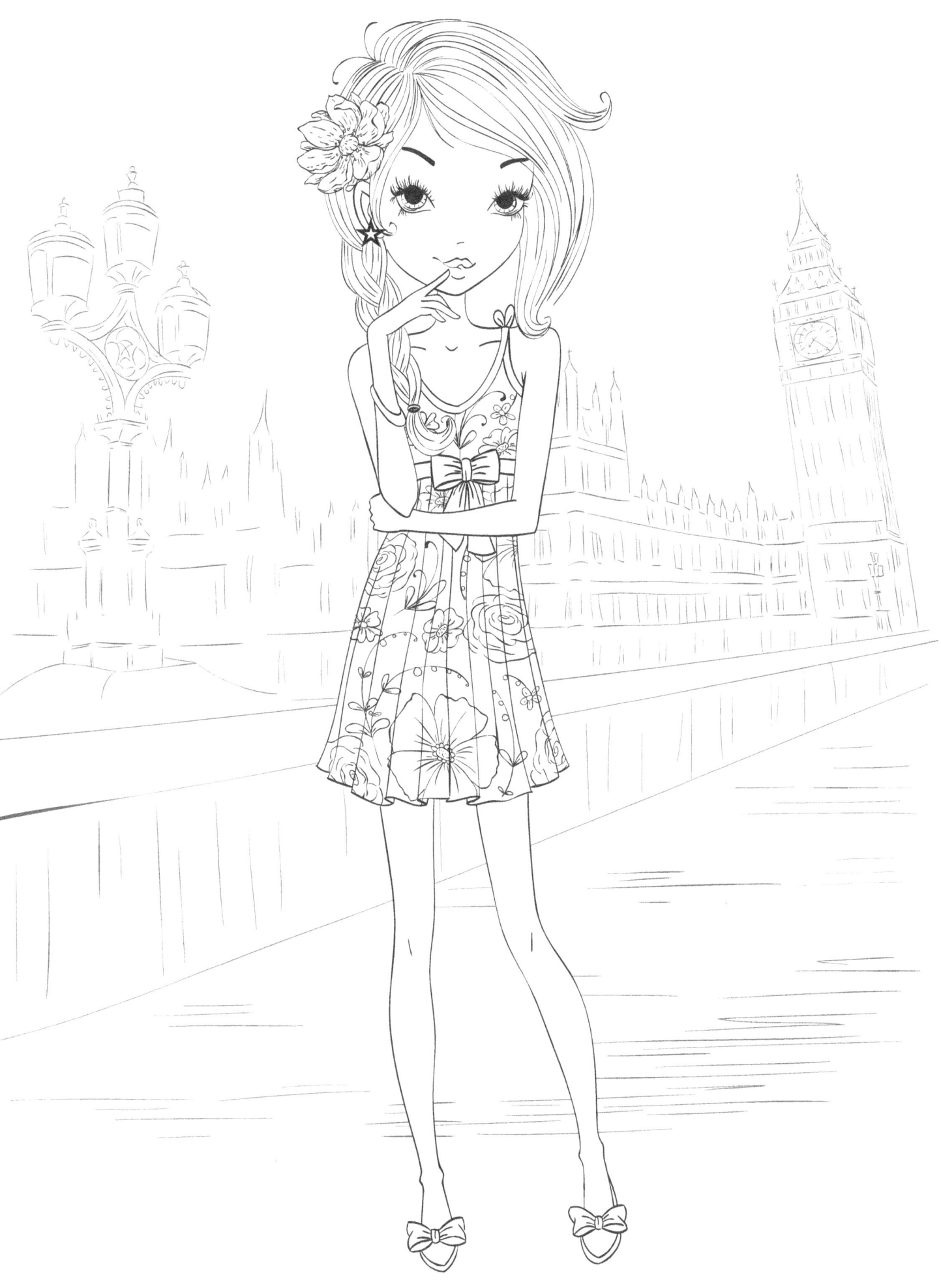

FASHION
Girl

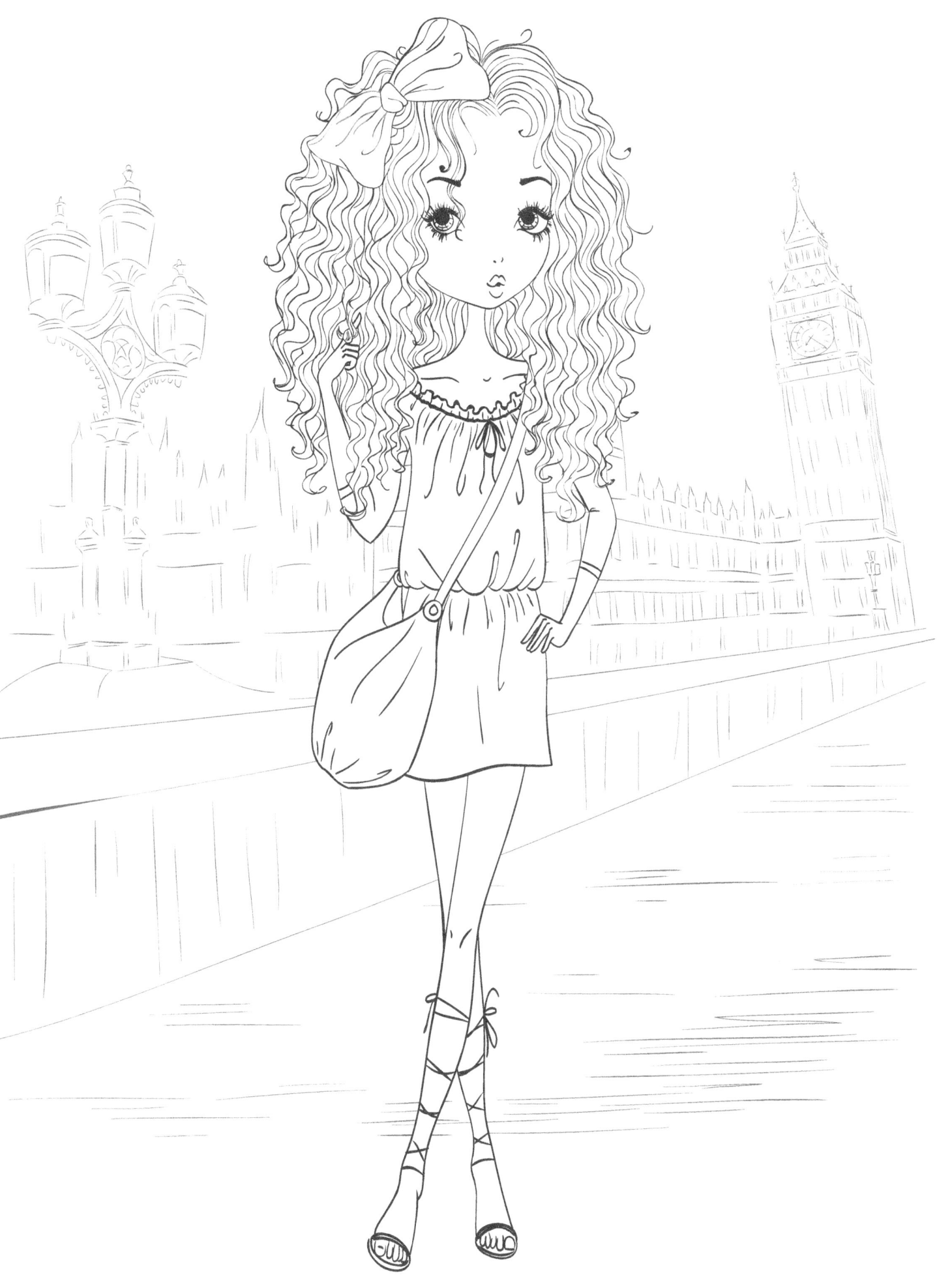

I ♡ my bike

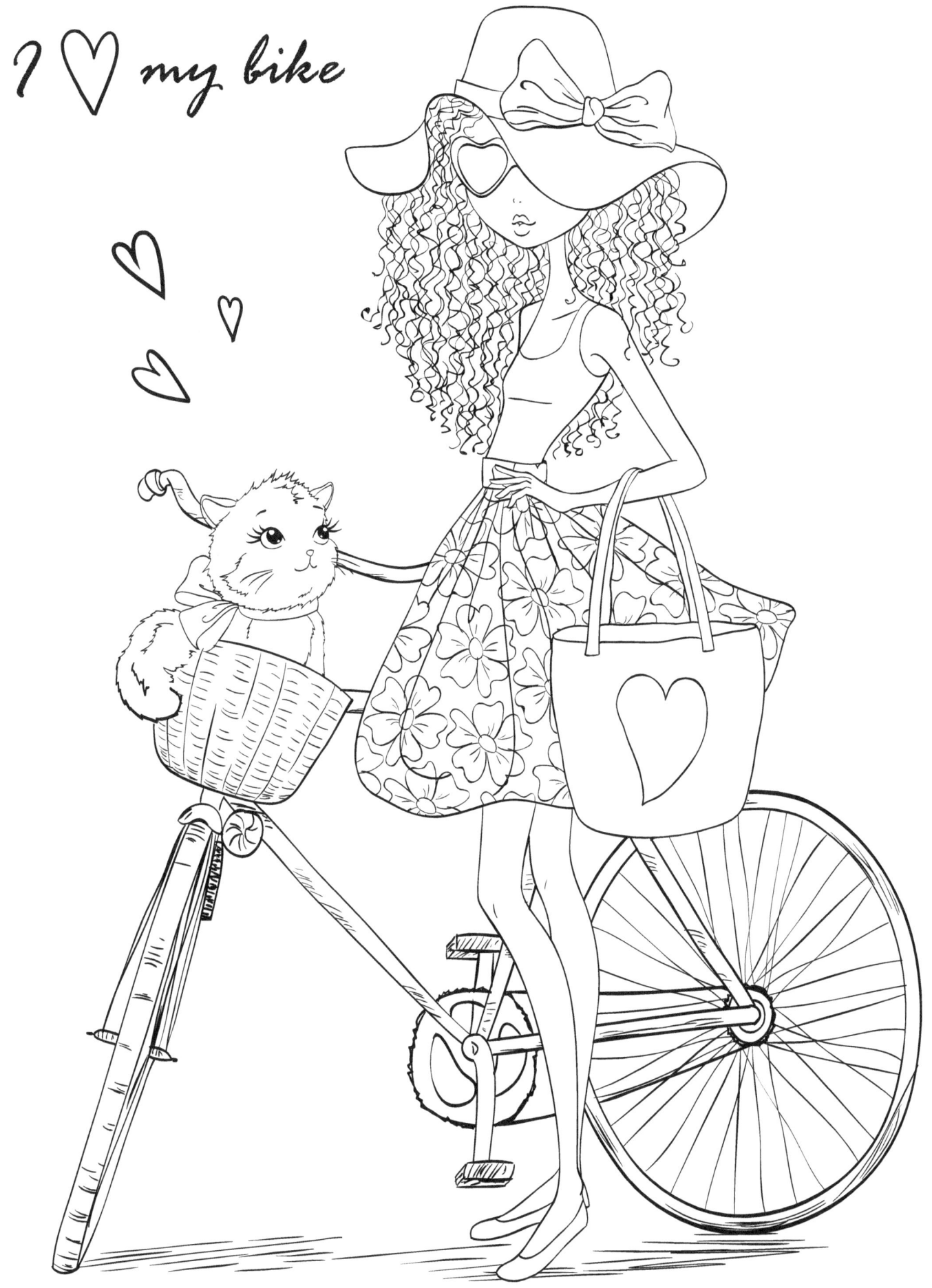

best friends

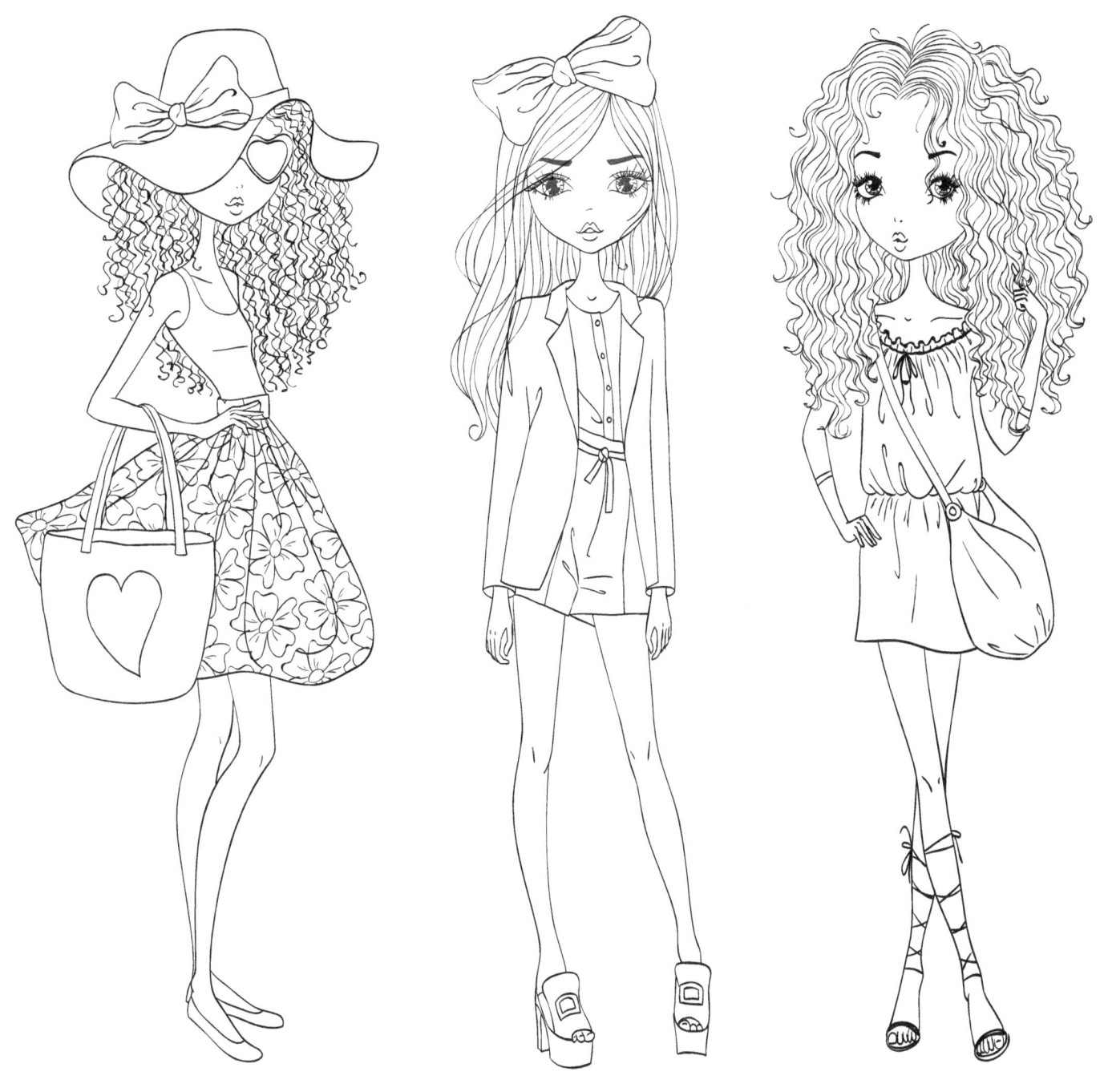

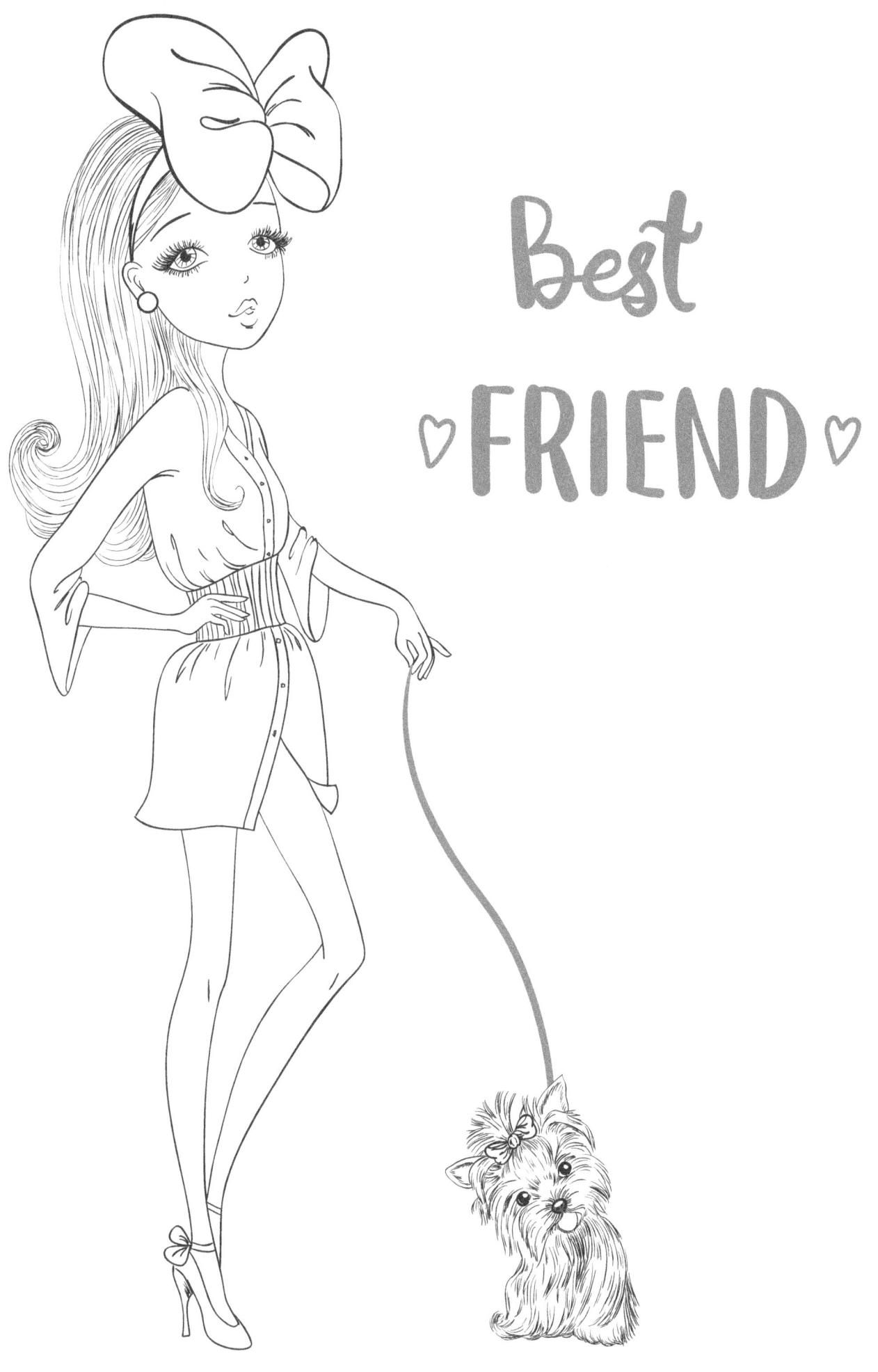

Best
FRIEND

Coloring Book for Tweens
Fashion Girls

Published by:
Art Therapy Coloring
www.arttherapycoloring.com

www.ingramcontent.com/pod-product-compliance
Lightning Source LLC
Chambersburg PA
CBHW081342180526
45171CB00006B/587